The Diary of Hannibal Barca

A Chronological Retrospect Centered on Polybius' Histories III

Hutan Ashrafian

DEDICATION

To my wonderful wife Leanne and delightful son Persie.

CONTENTS

ACKNOWLEDGMENTS

The calculated chronology of the diary here-in has been scaffolded onto the original English translation of Volume III of the Histories of Polybius by W. R. Paton (1922).

META-CHRONOLOGY SERIES PREFACE

There seems to be a grand disparity in the world of historians. Whilst the concept of history is relatively robust in society, there is a rift between *Modern* and *Ancient* Historians. Such a dichotomy seems to be artificial, for both study events in the past and both are aim to apply as much objectivity as possible to clarify the causal determinants of past effects; and as a result, to educate and inform contemporaneous society of these facts; ideally to minimize future societal mistakes and to guide beneficial future decisions. Nevertheless, the dichotomy between Ancient and Modern historians seems a pervading distinction that seems largely driven by the very nature of the sources each group has to study.

For example, a very modern historian may have access to *real-time* notes, emails, newspaper articles, television interviews, social media yield and a whole trench of other online media that are contextualized by major world timelines or a *macro-chronology* (such as leadership eras and major calendar events) in addition to a micro-chronology (specific day-to-day, hour-by-hour, minute-by-minute or even second-by-second events). Conversely, an ancient historian may have a few 2nd or 3rd hand sources written in an archaic language, sometimes many centuries after the occurrence of ancient events that predominantly only offer macro-chronological information. Such differences not only seem to affect the analysis of the past but also our interpretation. This seems to limit the interpretation of ancient sources that are treated as having a miasma of 2nd hand source bias, which is not considered to equate with the presumed clarity of modern sources due to their lack of an accepted micro-chronology of events.

My goal therefore has been to offer a micro-chronology of ancient events or an acuity of day-to-day real-time actuality to some ancient individuals and subjects. The integration between both macro- and micro-chronological views can therefore act as a method to cut through the presumed miasma of ancient sources. Sometimes it seems that studying ancient sources offers an encylopaedic appreciation of past events, but this may be tinted with a tone and timing that has a rather ethereal flavor rather than the likely reality of day-to-day events; which were just as real thousands of years ago as they are today. Studying the ancients without the cloak of romanticism, but rather one of scientific daily chronology may offer the reader of ancient sources the context of real-time impetus in decisions and actions. By doing so, it will allow the conceptual bridging of how ancient subjects were actually subjects living in another time, but nonetheless human subjects with comparative sentience and intelligence to their ancient contemporaries in the context of their day-to-day events.

The *real politic* of yester-year was just as real 20,000 years ago as it is today. Sometimes assessing ancient events devoid of time or place can lead to exaggeration and bias, particularly through each iteration of news dissemination. This is one source from which legends can come to exist; for example, there may have been a skirmish between several Mediterranean states and their leaders, which in today's world would be viewed as simply that. The same story devoid of time and place could lead to embellishment to scale in the time of events and size of actions. One could see the origins of Homer's Trojan Wars with demi-gods such as Achilles and magical depictions of Olympian Gods participating in human events. It is interesting to note that Homer by himself may have been aware of loss of time information, for there is a symmetrical chronology of events in the Iliad with times taking from one night to nine nights then to twelve nights then to one night then twelve nights and so on. Additionally the journey of the Odyssey is identical to that of the Trojan War in the Iliad, both ten years; though Odysseus' journey should only take the order of weeks. This likely synthetic approximation of time detracts form the reality of activity that in turn can spawn disinformation. Other examples include those of the Sumerian King List; here we know that some of the kings in this list existed, but clearly their reign length, some at 36,000 years is clearly unfeasible and has obscured analysis of Sumerian regnal time and events.

One classical example at an attempt to quantify the chronology of the past is that of Archbishop James Ussher (1581 – 1656). As a cleric, he expressed his deep devotion to the Bible by considering it as an incontrovertibly factual document. He applied scientific arithmetic to calculate his eponymous Chronology identifing the age of the world according to that text. Others such as Lightfoot, Ben Halafta, Bede and Newton also tried to create their own chronology. Independent to the consideration of the text in question, these attempts offered a quantifiable list of events by which to compare other models of chronology for ancient occurrences and offered a yardstick for which to allow a deeper timeline scrutiny for past events.

It is with this notion, that I have studied the ancient sources for prevailing characters from the ancient world and added a diary-like chronology to them for this 'Meta-Chronology' series (integrating both macro- and micro-chronology) on the most studied events of the most prominent ancient leaders (including the life and leadership of Alexander the Great and Xenophon's Anabasis who of interest where students of amongst the greatest philosophers of all time, Alexander-Aristotle and Xenophon-

Socrates). By doing so I aim to discard the shackles of '*Ancient vs. Modern*' or '*Legendary vs. Contemporary*', but rather to offer anyone interested a common chronological yardstick by which to cover both modern and ancient world events. Here, metaphorically, I have aimed to clarify the nature of each individual's timeline in the same vein that the *Alexander Mosaic* has been reconstructed to give the viewer a sense of its completeness of the original piece of art. Whilst I am aware there may be some inaccuracies in this method, I feel that the bigger picture may offer a stronger sense of existence in the characters discussed, particularly to give a feel of the urgency in decisions and actions as well as times of inaction. A method therefore to directly compare their ancient world with the modern one.

For these works, I have utilised accounts from established ancient sources on day-to-day activities of individuals and have super-imposed a *real-time* date on to those known events. To do this, I calculated specific days using set-dates from accepted or validated known-time points existing in the history of each individual and imputing of extrapolating the remaining dates in an individuals life based on the ancient sources in the texts listed. On occasion I have also imputed some figures based on the description of times, places and travel times (for example if it took 10 days to march from A to B and the distance form C to D resembles that of A to B and the journey speed or impetus was similar then I deduced the journey time would also follow). I have also added to the translation of ancient-to-modern chronology by converting ancient seasons into their modern ones through conversion of the ancient dates into their Julian calendar counterpart. For consistency, I have applied the Julian Calendar in year-month-day (YMD) format. For clarification of my personal comments in the text, I have utilized curly braces {}. These have been used to include relevant travel distances, travel information and the coupling of ancient locations to their current or hypothesized modern-day counterparts. Furthermore, where necessary, other sources have been utlised to clarify dates and events. Specifically for lunar, solar, or astronomical data, sources from NASA (National Aeronautics and Space Administration) or accepted modern astronomical tables/software (including Alcyone) have been applied.

In this series, I have also categorized the listed ancient dates according to modern day designations (Sunday to Saturday utilizing the Computer Support Group [CSGNetwork.com] Calendar Converter and Translator). Whilst these days are based on a cyclical mathematical progression that is arbitrary (these day names did not exist in ancient times) and do not take into account the many calendars (of differing lengths, months and days) applied in the ancient world, the robustness of a continuous mathematically calculated sequential seven day system allows the reader to discern any seven day trends that may have occurred in the chronology of the book. For example, if person A went to war on Monday August 5th in one year and had a celebratory feast on a Monday in August the next year, this may offer an insight regarding the timing and association between these two events. Possibly the 'Monday' or that day in a rolling calendar represented something of note. Additionally it offers the reader an additional sense of tangibility and context within the modern-world calendar timeframe regarding events that occurred thousands of years ago. Significantly however, this *virtual diary* format does carry some limitations. The dates listed are not fact but calculations aiming to offer the most likely factual times. As a result, they cannot be taken as verbatim, but rather they represent the best educated guess as to when the specified ancient events actually took place.

My ultimate aim is therefore to offer a deeper perception of *'real-time'* for ancient events that to-date have suffered from being morphed to exist in an abstract space-time of their own devoid of scale and measure. It is with this I wish the reader a tangibly timely appreciation of ancient historical events.

Hutan Ashrafian
Primrose Hill, London
2017

PREFACE

Hannibal Barca is considered amongst the greatest military leaders of all time. According to some military strategists, his tactics remain the most applicable to modern-day warfare and have endured more than that of any other leader from the ancient world.

Although he is not given the epithet of 'The Great', this is likely due to the fact that he did not end his life having amassed a large geographical or political empire. Rather, he died having lived on the reputation of his first 5 years in power. Over this time he had found himself progressing from the position of military general without significant support from his own nation (Carthage) to a position where he could conceivably crush and invade the world's greatest empire (Rome).

If this was not enough, he had achieved such a feat by creating an alliance of multi-lingual, multi-ethnic groups who, despite language barriers, performed one of military history's greatest and most unpredictable journeys across the Alps. Furthermore, he survived and defeated the Romans in their 'own back yard' of Italy.

These events culminated in Rome's greatest defeat at the battle of Cannae, swiftly followed by the question of why Hannibal did not invade Rome itself after such an astonishing success. It has been widely speculated that had such an invasion taken place, the current world in which we live would have been very different, and may have even been based on its Carthaginian language equivalent with our education, philosophy, architecture, science, and art derived from a predominantly North African culture (rather than on the precepts and culture of the Roman *Res publica*). In reality however, Hannibal's decision not to invade Rome was most likely based on his understanding that the magnitude and complexity of such an invasion would have been technically unmanageable for his forces.

Following this, for the remainder of Hannibal's life he followed continued lesser military campaigns with little success. Most notably was his defeat against Publius Cornelius Scipio Africanus (236–183 BC) who, with the power of the Roman empire behind him, proved a brilliant and cunning rival. Subsequently, upon being exiled Hannibal ultimately became a form of 'military consultant' utilising his reputation as a victory trophy. His exact cause of death remains uncertain although it is thought to be either the result of an accidental self-inflicted wound or self-poisoning to elude capture by his Roman enemies.

During the period of the 140th Olympiad, Hannibal enjoyed a number of astounding military successes. During the *'anni mirabiles'* from 221-226 BC he not only crossed the Alps but also won the battles of Trebia, Trasimene and Cannae. Had he died at this time, it is likely that he would have been titled 'Hannibal the Great'. Yet, he continued his struggle against the Roman empire for approximately another three-and-a-half decades until the age of 64-66.

The aim of this book is to present the timeline of Hannibal's *anni mirabiles* corresponding to Book III of *The Histories* by Polybius. These have been scaffolded onto the corresponding English text translated originally by W. R. Paton (1922). Where times or durations are not explicitly stated, time lengths have been imputed from the text. Where this has not been possible, realistic travel times have been calculated from other comparable times in the text and additional context from a strategic military viewpoint added. The conversion of all dates into the Julian Calendar has been applied (the predominant method of assessing ancient sources with consistency), as this will allow the easiest assessment of time comparisons within the modern world. Such an analysis allows for a more detailed interpretation of his greatest achievements and the context with which they occurred. It is hoped that the diary format of the text will offer the reader a better appreciation of Hannibal's decisions, strategies, and leadership choices in some of the greatest military exploits of all time.

Hutan Ashrafian
Primrose Hill, London
2017

1 PRELUDE

1 In my first Book, the third, that is, from this counting backwards, I explained that I fixed as the starting-points of my work, the Social war, the Hannibalic war, and the war for Coele-Syria. I likewise set forth in the same place the reasons why I wrote the two preceding Books dealing with events of an earlier date. I will now attempt to give a well attested account of the above wars, their first causes and the reasons why they attained such magnitude; but in the first place I have a few words to say regarding my work as a whole.

The subject I have undertaken to treat, the how, when, and wherefore of the subjection of the known parts of the world to the dominion of Rome, should be viewed as a single whole, with a recognized beginning, a fixed duration, and an end which is not a matter of dispute; and I think it will be advantageous to give a brief prefatory survey of the chief parts of this whole from the beginning to the end. For I believe this will be the best means of giving students an adequate idea of my whole plan. Since a previous general view is of great assistance to the mind in acquiring a knowledge of details, and at the same time a previous notion of the details helps us to knowledge of the whole, I regard a preliminary survey based on both as best and will draw up these prefatory remarks to my history on this principle. I have already indicated the general scope and limits of this history. The particular events comprised in it begin with the above-mentioned wars and culminate and end in the destruction of the Macedonian monarchy. Between the beginning and end lies a space of fifty-three years, comprising a greater number of grave and momentous events than any period of equal length in the past. Starting from the 140th Olympiad I shall adopt the following order in my exposition of them.

2 First I shall indicate the causes of the above war between Rome and Carthage, known as the Hannibalic war, and tell how the Carthaginians invaded Italy, broke up the dominion of Rome, and cast the Romans into great fear for their safety and even for their native soil, while great was their own hope, such as they had never dared to entertain, of capturing Rome itself. Next I shall attempt to describe how at the same period Philip of Macedon, after finishing his war with the Aetolians and settling the affairs of Greece, conceived the project of an alliance with Carthage; how Antiochus and Ptolemy Philopator first quarrelled and at length went to war with each other for the possession of Coele-Syria, and how the Rhodians and Prusias, declaring war on the Byzantines, compelled them to stop levying toll on ships bound for the Euxine. Interrupting my narrative at this point, I shall draw up my account of the Roman Constitution, as a sequel to which I shall point out how the peculiar qualities of the Constitution conduced very largely not only to their subjection of the Italians and Sicilians, and subsequently of the Spaniards and Celts, but finally to their victory over Carthage and their conceiving the project of universal empire. Simultaneously in a digression I shall narrate how the dominion of Hiero of Syracuse fell and after this I shall deal with the troubles in Egypt, and tell how, on the death of Ptolemy, Antiochus and Philip, conspiring to partition the dominions of his son, a helpless infant, began to be guilty of acts of unjust aggression, Philip laying hands on the islands of the Aegean, and on Caria and Samos, while Antiochus seized on Coele-Syria and Phoenicia.

3 Next, after summing up the doings of the Romans and Carthaginians in Spain, Africa, and Sicily I shall shift the scene of my story definitely, as the scene of action shifted, to Greece and its neighbourhood. I shall describe the sea-battles in which Attalus and the Rhodians met Philip, and after this deal with the war between the Romans and Philip, its course, its reason, and its result. Following on this I shall make mention of the angry spirit of the Aetolians yielding to which they invited Antiochus over, and thus set ablaze the war from Asia against the Achaeans and Romans. After narrating the causes of this war, and how Antiochus crossed to Europe, I shall describe in the first place how he fled from Greece; secondly how on his defeat after this he abandoned all Asia up to the Taurus; and thirdly, how the Romans, suppressing the insolence of the Galatian Gauls, established their undisputed supremacy in Asia and freed its inhabitants on this side of the Taurus from the fear of barbarians and the lawless violence of these Gauls. Next I shall bring before the reader's eyes the misfortune that befel the Aetolians and Cephallenians, and then make mention of the war of Eumenes with Prusias and the Gauls and of that between Ariarathes and Pharnaces. Subsequently, after some notice of the unification and pacification of the Peloponnese and of the growth of the Rhodian State, I shall bring the whole narrative of events to a conclusion, narrating finally the expedition of Antiochus Epiphanes against Egypt, the war with Perseus, and the abolition of the Macedonian monarchy. All the above events will enable us to perceive how the Romans dealt with each contingency and thus subjected the whole world to their rule.

4 Now if from their success or failure alone we could form an adequate judgement of how far states and individuals are worthy of praise or blame, I could here lay down my pen, bringing my narrative and this whole work to a close with the last-mentioned events, as was my original intention. For the period of fifty-three years finished here, and the growth and advance of Roman power was now complete. Besides which it was now universally accepted as a necessary fact that henceforth all must submit to the Romans and obey their orders. But since judgements regarding either the conquerors or the conquered based purely on performance are by no means final — what is thought to be the greatest success having brought the greatest calamities on many, if they do not make proper use of it, and the most dreadful catastrophes often turning out to the advantage of those who support them bravely — I must append to the history of the above period an account of the subsequent policy of the conquerors and their method of universal rule, as well as of the various opinions and appreciations of their rulers entertained by the subjects, and finally I must describe what were the prevailing and dominant tendencies and ambitions of the various peoples in their private and public life. For it is evident that contemporaries will thus be able to see clearly whether the Roman rule is acceptable or the reverse, and future generations whether their government should be considered to have been worthy of praise and admiration or rather of blame. And indeed it is just in this that the chief usefulness of this work for the present and the future will lie. For neither rulers themselves nor their critics should regard the end of action as being merely conquest and the subjection of all to their rule; since no man of sound sense goes to war with his neighbours simply for the sake of crushing an adversary, just as no one sails on the open sea just for the sake of crossing it. Indeed no one even takes up the study of arts and crafts merely for the sake of knowledge, but all men do all they do for the resulting pleasure, good, or utility. So the final end achieved by this work will be, to gain knowledge of what was the condition of each people after all had been crushed and had come under the dominion of Rome, until the disturbed and troubled time that afterwards ensued. About this latter, owing to the importance of the actions and the unexpected character of the events, and chiefly because I not only witnessed most but took part and even directed some, I was induced to write as if starting on a fresh work.

5 This period of disturbance comprises, firstly the war waged by Rome against the Celtiberians and Vaccaei, that between Carthage and Massinissa the King of the Libyans and that between Attalus and Prusias in Asia. Next, Ariarathes, King of Cappadocia was expelled from his kingdom by Orophernes through the agency of King Demetrius and recovered his ancestral throne by the help of Attalus. Then Demetrius, son of Seleucus, after reigning in Syria for twelve years lost both his kingdom and his life, the other kings combining against him. Next the Romans restored to their homes the Greeks who had been accused in consequence of the war with Perseus, acquitting them of the charges brought against them. A little later the Romans attacked Carthage, having resolved in the first place on changing its site and subsequently on its utter destruction for the reasons that I shall state in due course. Close upon this followed the withdrawal of the Macedonians from their alliance with Rome and that of the Lacedaemonians from the Achaean League, and hereupon the beginning and the end of the general calamity that overtook Greece.

Such is the plan I propose, but all depends on Fortune's granting me a life long enough to execute it. However I am convinced that in the event of my death, the project will not fall to the ground for want of men competent to carry it on, since there are many others who will set their hands to the task and labour to complete it.

Now having given a summary of the most important events, with the object of conveying to my readers a notion of this work as a whole and its contents in detail, it is time for me to call to mind my original plan and return to the starting-point of my history.

6 Some of those authors who have dealt with Hannibal and his times, wishing to indicate the causes that led to the above war between Rome and Carthage, allege as its first cause the siege of Saguntum by the Carthaginians and as its second their crossing, contrary to treaty, the river whose native name is the Iber. I should agree in stating that these were the beginnings of the war, but I can by no means allow that they were its causes, unless we call Alexander's crossing to Asia the cause of his war against Persia and Antiochus' landing at Demetrias the cause of his war against Rome, neither of which assertions is either reasonable or true. For who could consider these to be causes of wars, plans and preparations for which, in the case of the Persian war, had been made earlier, many by Alexander and even some by Philip during his life, and in the case of the war against Rome by the Aetolians long before Antiochus arrived? These are pronouncements of men who are unable to see the great and essential distinction between a beginning and a cause or purpose, these being the first origin of all, and the

4

beginning coming last. By the beginning of something I mean the first attempt to execute and put in action plans on which we have decided, by its causes what is most initiatory in our judgements and opinions, that is to say our notions of things, our state of mind, our reasoning about these, and everything through which we reach decisions and projects. The nature of these is evident from the instances adduced above; it is easy for anyone to see the real causes and origin of the war against Persia. The first was the retreat of the Greeks under Xenophon from the upper Satrapies, in which, though they traversed the whole of Asia, a hostile country, none of the barbarians ventured to face them. The second was the crossing of Agesilaus, King of Sparta, to Asia, where he found no opposition of any moment to his projects, and was only compelled to return without effecting anything owing to the disturbances in Greece. From both of these facts Philip perceived and reckoned on the cowardice and indolence of the Persians as compared with the military efficiency of himself and his Macedonians, and further fixing his eyes on the splendour of the great prize which the war promised, he lost no time, once he had secured the avowed good-will of the Greeks, but seizing on the pretext that it was his urgent duty to take vengeance on the Persians for their injurious treatment of the Greeks, he bestirred himself and decided to go to war, beginning to make every preparation for this purpose. We must therefore look on the first considerations I have mentioned as the causes of the war against Persia, the second as its pretext and Alexander's crossing to Asia as its beginning.

7 Similarly it is evident that the cause of the war between Antiochus and the Romans was the anger of the Aetolians, who (as I above stated) looking upon themselves as having been slighted in many ways by the Romans as regards their share in bringing the war with Philip to an end, not only invited Antiochus over, but were ready to do and suffer anything owing to the anger they conceived under the above circumstances. But the liberation of Greece, which they announced in defiance of reason and truth going round with Antiochus from city to city, we must consider to be a pretext of this war, and its beginning the landing of Antiochus at Demetrias.

In speaking at such length on this matter, my object has not been to censure previous writers, but to rectify the ideas of students. For of what use to the sick is a physician who is ignorant of the causes of certain conditions of the body? And of what use is a statesman who cannot reckon how, why, and whence each event has originated? The former will scarcely be likely to recommend proper treatment for the body and it will be impossible for the latter without such knowledge to deal properly with circumstances. Nothing, therefore, should be more carefully guarded against and more diligently sought out than the first causes of each event, since matters of the greatest moment often originate from trifles, and it is the initial impulses and conceptions in every matter which are most easily remedied.

8 Fabius, the Roman annalist, says that besides the outrage on the Saguntines, a cause of the war was Hasdrubal's ambition and love of power. He tells us how, having acquired a great dominion in Spain, he arrived in Africa and attempted to abolish the constitution of Carthage and change the form of government to a monarchy. The leading statesmen, however, got wind of his project and united to oppose him, upon which Hasdrubal, suspicious of their intentions, left Africa and in future governed Iberia as he chose, without paying any attention to the Carthaginian Senate. Hannibal from boyhood had shared and admired Hasdrubal's principles; and on succeeding to the governor-generalship of Iberia, he had employed the same method as Hasdrubal. Consequently, he now began this war against Rome on his own initiative and in defiance of Carthaginian opinion, not a single one of the notables in Carthage approving his conduct towards Saguntum. After telling us this, Fabius says that on the capture of this city the Romans came forward demanding that the Carthaginians should either deliver Hannibal into their hands or accept war. Now if anyone were to pose the following question to this writer — how opportunity could have better favoured the Carthaginians' wishes or what could have been a juster act and more in their interest (since, as he says, they had disapproved Hannibal's action from the outset) than to yield to the Roman demand, and by giving up the man who had caused the offence, with some show of reason to destroy by the hands of others the common enemy of their state and secure the safety of their territory, ridding themselves of the war that menaced them and accomplishing their vengeance by a simple resolution — if anyone, I say, were to ask him this, what would he have to say? Evidently nothing; for so far were they from doing any of the above things that after carrying on the war, in obedience to Hannibal's decision, for seventeen years, they did not abandon the struggle, until finally, every resource on which they relied being now exhausted, their native city and her inhabitants stood in deadly peril.

9 One may ask why I make any mention of Fabius and his statement. It is not from apprehension lest it may find acceptance from some owing to its plausibility; for its inherent unreasonableness, even without my comment, is self-evident to anyone who reads it. But what I wish is to warn those who consult his books not to pay attention to the title, but to facts. For there are some people who pay regard not to what he writes but to the writer himself and, taking into consideration that he was a contemporary and a Roman senator, at once accept all he says as worthy of credit. But my own opinion is that while not treating his authority as negligible we should not regard it as final, but that readers should in most cases test his statements by reference to the actual facts.

To return to the war between Rome and Carthage, from which this digression has carried us away, we must regard its first cause as being the indignation of Hamilcar surnamed Barcas, the actual father of Hannibal. Unvanquished in spirit by the war for Sicily, since he felt that he had kept the army of Eryx under his command combative and resolute until the end, and had only agreed to peace yielding to circumstances after the defeat of the Carthaginians in the naval battle, he maintained his resolve and waited for an opportunity to strike. Had not the mutinous outbreak among the mercenaries occurred, he would very soon, as far as it lay in his power, have created some other means and other resources for resuming the contest, but he was hampered by these civil disturbances which occupied all his time and attention.

10 When, on the suppression of this disturbance by the Carthaginians, the Romans announced their intention of making war on Carthage, the latter at first was ready to negotiate on all points, thinking that, justice being on her side, she would prevail (about this I have spoken in the preceding Books, without a perusal of which it is impossible to follow properly what I am now saying and what I am about to say); but as the Romans refused to negotiate, the Carthaginians had to yield to circumstances, and though deeply aggrieved they were powerless, and evacuated Sardinia, agreeing also to pay twelve hundred talents in addition to the sum previously exacted, in order not to be forced to accept war at that time. This, then, we must take to be the second and principal cause of the subsequent war; for Hamilcar, with the anger felt by all his compatriots at this last outrage added to his old indignation, as soon as he had finally crushed the mutiny of the mercenaries and secured the safety of his country, at once threw all his efforts into the conquest of Spain, with the object of using the resources thus obtained for the war against Rome. This success of the Carthaginian project in Spain must be held to be the third cause of the war, for relying on this increase of strength, they entered upon it with confidence.

Of the fact that Hamilcar, although he died ten years before the beginning of the Second Punic War, contributed much to its origin many evidences can be found; but the anecdote I am about to relate suffices, I think, to confirm this.

11 At the time when Hannibal on his final defeat by the Romans had left his native land and was staying at the court of Antiochus, the Romans, who saw through the project of the Aetolians, sent an embassy to Antiochus, wishing to be fully aware what the king's purpose was. The legates, as they saw that Antiochus was lending an ear to the Aetolians and was disposed to go to war with Rome, paid many attentions to Hannibal, wishing to make Antiochus suspicious of him, as in fact they succeeded in doing. For as time went on, the king's mistrust of Hannibal grew ever more strong; and it fell out on one occasion that they came to have a talk about the alienation which had been secretly growing up between them. In the course of the conversation Hannibal defended himself on various grounds, and at length, being at a loss for further arguments, resorted to the following. He said that at the time when his father was about to start with his army on his expedition to Spain, he himself, then nine years of age, was standing by the altar, while Hamilcar was sacrificing to Zeus. When, on the omens being favourable, Hamilcar had poured a libation to the gods and performed all the customary rites, he ordered the others who were attending the sacrifice to withdraw to a slight distance and calling Hannibal to him asked him kindly if he wished to accompany him on the expedition. On his accepting with delight, and, like a boy, even begging to do it besides, his father took him by the hand, led him up to the altar, and bade him lay his hand on the victim and swear never to be the friend of the Romans. He begged Antiochus, then, now he knew this for a fact, as long as his intentions were hostile to Rome, to rely on him confidently and believe that he would have in him his sincerest supporter, but from the moment he made peace and alliance with her he had no need to wait for accusations but should mistrust and beware of him; for there was nothing he would not do against the Romans.

12 Antiochus, listening to this, thought he spoke genuinely and sincerely and in consequence abandoned all his former mistrust. However, we should consider this as an unquestionable proof of Hamilcar's hostility and general purpose, and it is confirmed by the facts. For he made of his daughter's husband Hasdrubal and his own son Hannibal such enemies of Rome that none could be more bitter. As Hasdrubal died before putting his purpose into execution, it was not in his case fully evident, but circumstance put it in the power of Hannibal to give only too manifest proof of his inherited hatred of Rome. Therefore, statesmen should above all take care that the true motives of the reconciliation of enmities and the formation of friendships do not escape them. They should observe when it is that men come to terms under pressure of circumstances and when owing to their spirit being broken, so that in the former case they may regard them as reserving themselves for a favourable opportunity and be constantly on their guard, and in the latter they may trust them as true friends and subjects and not hesitate to command their services when required.

We must consider, then, the causes of the Hannibalic War to have been those I have stated, while its beginnings were as follows.

221 BC (LEAP YEAR)

October 04, Saturday
The Death of Hasdrubal

13 The Carthaginians could ill bear their defeat in the war for Sicily, and, as I said above, they were additionally exasperated by the matter of Sardinia and the exorbitancy of the sum they had been last obliged to agree to pay. Therefore, when they had subjugated the greater part of Iberia, they were quite ready to adopt any measures against Rome which suggested themselves. On the death of Hasdrubal, to whom after that of Hamilcar they had entrusted the government of Iberia, they at first waited for a pronouncement on the part of the troops, and

October 13, Monday
News that Hannibal was voted as commander-in-chief of the Carthaginians

when news reached them from their armies that the soldiers had unanimously chosen Hannibal as their commander,

October 15, Wednesday
Carthaginian General Assembly ratifies Hannibal's position

they hastened to summon a general assembly of the commons, which unanimously ratified the choice of the soldiers.

October 19, Sunday
Hannibal assumes command of the Carthaginian army

Hannibal on assuming the command,

October 22, Wednesday
Commences campaign against the Olcades (corresponding to the modern-day modern province of Cuenca in Spain)

at once set forth with the view of subduing a tribe called the Olcades, and

October 26, Sunday
Arrives at Althaea (corresponding to the modern-day city of Los Villares)

arriving before their most powerful city Althaea, encamped there and soon made himself master of it by a series of vigorous and formidable assaults, upon which the rest of the tribe were overawed and submitted to the Carthaginians.

November 22, Saturday
Completes successful campaign against the Olcades

After exacting tribute from the towns and possessing himself of a considerable sum,

November 26, Wednesday
Sets up winter camp at New Carthage (corresponding to the modern-day city of Cartagena)

he retired to winter quarters at New Carthage. By the generosity he now displayed to the troops under his command, paying them in part and promising further payment, he inspired in them great good-will to himself and high hopes of the future.

220 BC

June 03, Wednesday
Commences summer campaigns

14 Next summer he made a fresh attack on the Vaccaei,

June 18, Thursday
Takes the city of Hermandica

assaulted and took Hermandica at the first onset,

June 30, Tuesday
Lays siege to the city of Arbacla

but Arbacala being a very large city with a numerous and brave population, he had to lay siege to it and

August 15, Saturday
Arbacla falls

only took it by assault after much pains.

August 26, Wednesday
Carpetani and the neighbouring tribes rise against the Carthaginians

Subsequently on his return he unexpectedly found himself in great peril, the Carpetani, the strongest tribe in the district gathering to attack him and being joined by the neighbouring tribes, all incited to this by the fugitive Olcades, and also by those who had escaped from Hermandica. Had the Carthaginians been obliged to meet all this host in a pitched battle, they would assuredly have suffered defeat; but, as it was,

September 03, Thursday
Retreats on the other side of the Tagus river

Hannibal very wisely and skilfully faced about and retreated so as to place the river Tagus in his front, and remained there to dispute the crossing, availing himself of the aid both of the river and of his elephants, of which he had about forty, so that everything went as he had calculated and as no one else would have dared to expect.

September 12, Saturday
Carpetani alliance attack

For when the barbarians tried to force a crossing at various points, the greater mass of them perished in coming out of the river, the elephants following its bank and being upon them as soon as they landed. Many also were cut down in the stream itself by the cavalry, as the horses could bear up better against the current, and the mounted men in fighting had the advantage of being higher than the unmounted enemy.

September 17, Thursday
Defeats the Carpetani alliance

Finally, Hannibal in his turn crossed the river and attacked the barbarians, putting to flight a force of more than one hundred thousand.

September 19, Saturday

After their defeat none of the peoples on that side of the Ebro ventured lightly to face the Carthaginians, with the exception of the Saguntines. Hannibal tried as far as he could to keep his hands off this city, wishing to give the Romans no avowed pretext for war, until he had secured his possession of all the rest of the country, following in this his father

Hamilcar's suggestions and advice.

October

15 But the Saguntines sent repeated messages to Rome, as on the one hand they were alarmed for their own safety and foresaw what was coming, and at the same time they wished to keep the Romans informed how well things went with the Carthaginians in Spain.

November 19, Thursday
Romans send legates to report on Saguntum

The Romans, who had more than once paid little attention to them, sent on this occasion legates to report on the situation.

December 07, Monday
Arrival at New Carthage for the winter

Hannibal at the same time, having reduced the tribes he intended, arrived with his forces to winter at New Carthage, which was in a way the chief ornament and capital of the Carthaginian empire in Spain.

December 08, Tuesday
Disagreement with the Roman legates

Here he found the Roman legates, to whom he gave audience and listened to their present communication. The Romans protested against his attacking Saguntum, which they said was under their protection, or crossing the Ebro, contrary to the treaty engagements entered into in Hasdrubal's time. Hannibal, being young, full of martial ardour, encouraged by the success of his enterprises, and spurred on by his long-standing enmity to Rome, in his answer to the legates affected to be guarding the interests of the Saguntines and accused the Romans of having a short time previously, when there was a party quarrel at Saguntum and they were called in to arbitrate, unjustly put to death some of the leading men. The Carthaginians, he said, would not overlook this violation of good faith for it was from of old the principle of Carthage never to neglect the cause of the victims of injustice.

December 09, Wednesday
Sends message to Carthage to ask for plans regarding Saguntum

To Carthage, however, he sent, asking for instructions, since the Saguntines, relying on their alliance with Rome, were wronging some of the peoples subject to Carthage. Being wholly under the influence of unreasoning and violent anger, he did not allege the true reasons, but took refuge in groundless pretexts, as men are wont to do who disregard duty because they are prepossessed by passion. How much better would it have been for him to demand from the Romans the restitution of Sardinia, and at the same time of the tribute which they had so unjustly exacted, availing themselves of the misfortunes of Carthage, and to threaten war in the event of refusal! But as it was, by keeping silent as to the real cause and by inventing a non-existing one about Saguntum, he gave the idea that he was entering on the war not only unsupported by reason but without justice on his side.

December 12, Saturday
Roman legates go directly to Carthage

The Roman legates, seeing clearly that war was inevitable, took ship for Carthage to convey the same protest to the Government there. They never thought, however, that the war would be in Italy, but supposed they would fight in Spain with Saguntum for a base.

16 Consequently, the Senate, adapting their measures to this supposition, decided to secure their position in Illyria, as they foresaw that the war would be serious and long and the scene of it far away from home. It so happened that at that time in Illyria Demetrius of Pharos, oblivious of the benefits that the Romans had conferred on him, contemptuous of Rome because of the peril to which she was exposed first from the Gauls and now from Carthage, and placing all his hopes in the Royal House of Macedon owing to his having fought by the side of Antigonus in the battles against Cleomenes, was sacking and destroying the Illyrian cities subject to Rome, and, sailing beyond Lissus, contrary to the terms of the treaty, with fifty boats, had pillaged many of the Cyclades. The Romans, in view of those proceedings and of the flourishing fortunes of the Macedonian kingdom, were anxious to secure their position in the lands lying east of Italy, feeling confident that they would have time to correct the errors of the Illyrians and rebuke and chastise Demetrius for his ingratitude and temerity. But in this calculation they were deceived.

219 BC

May 23, Sunday
Hannibal leaves to lay siege to Saguntum (at the time when Lucius Aemilius was sent to Illyria; just before the rising of the Pleiades that year in 219 BC on the 25th May)

for Hannibal forestalled them by taking Saguntum, and, as a consequence, the war was not waged in Spain but at the very gates of Rome and through the whole of Italy. However, the Romans now moved by these considerations dispatched a force under Lucius Aemilius just before summer in the first year of the 140th Olympiad to operate in Illyria.

17 Hannibal at the same time quitted New Carthage with his army and advanced towards Saguntum. This city lies on the seaward foot of the range of hills connecting Iberia and Celtiberia, at a distance of about seven stades from the sea. The territory of the Saguntines yields every kind of crop and is the most fertile in the whole of Iberia. Hannibal, now encamping before the town, set himself to besiege it vigorously, foreseeing that many advantages would result from its capture. First of all he thought that he would thus deprive the Romans of any prospect of a campaign in Iberia, and secondly he was convinced that by this blow he would inspire universal terror, and render the Iberian tribes who had already submitted more orderly and those who were still independent more cautious, while above all he would be enabled to advance safely with no enemy left in his rear. Besides, he would then have abundant funds and supplies for his projected expedition, he would raise the spirit of his troops by the booty distributed among them and would conciliate the Carthaginians at home by the spoils he would send them. From all these considerations he actively pursued the siege, now setting an example to the soldiers by sharing personally the fatigue of the battering operations, now cheering on the troops and exposing recklessly to danger.

August 13, Friday
Hannibal conquers Saguntum after eight months (much debate has arisen by this timing. The majority of historians to-date have considered the Saguntum event as an eight month siege, which if commenced in May 219 would end in January 218 BC. This chronology does not fit the timing below that the Romans found out about the fall of the city in summer. The author interprets the eight month period from when Hannibal had considered the issue of Saguntum formally from the time he met the Roman legates. This would then allow for (i) an overall period of 8 months and (ii) the timing of the Romans hearing of the fall in late summer, with (iii) Hannibal having started the siege in early summer)

At length after eight months of hardship and anxiety he took the city by storm. A great booty of money, slaves, and property fell into his hands. The money, as he had determined, he set aside for his own purposes, the slaves he distributed among his men according to rank, and the miscellaneous property he sent off at once to Carthage. The result did not deceive his expectations, nor did he fail to accomplish his original purpose; but he both made his troops more eager to face danger and the Carthaginians more ready to accede to his demands on them, while he himself, by setting aside these funds, was able to accomplish many things of much service to him.

18 While this was taking place Demetrius, getting wind of the Romans' purpose, at once sent a considerable garrison to Dimale with the supplies requisite for such a force. In the other cities he made away with those who opposed his policy and placed the government in the hands of his friends while he himself, selecting six thousand of his bravest troops, quartered them at Pharos. The Roman Consul, on reaching Illyria with his army and observing that the enemy were very confident in the natural strength of Dimale and the measures they had taken for its defence, there being also a general belief that it was impregnable, decided to attack it first, wishing to strike terror into them. Having given instructions to his officers and erected batteries in several places he began to besiege it. By capturing it in seven days, he at one blow broke the spirit of all the enemy, so that from every city they at once flocked to surrender themselves unconditionally to Rome. Having accepted their submission and imposed suitable conditions on each he sailed to Pharos to attack Demetrius himself. Learning that the city was very strong, that a large force of exceptionally fine troops was assembled within it and that it was excellently furnished with supplies and munitions of war, he was apprehensive that the siege might prove difficult and long. In view of this, therefore, he employed the following impromptu stratagem. Sailing up to the island at night with his whole force he disembarked the greater part of it in certain well-wooded dells, and at daybreak with twenty ships sailed openly against the harbour which lies nearest to the town. Demetrius, seeing the ships and contemptuous of their small number, sallied from the city down to the harbour to prevent the enemy from landing. On his encountering them

19 the struggle was very violent, and more and more troops kept coming out of the town to help, until at length the whole garrison had poured out to take part in the battle. The Roman force which had landed in the night now opportunely arrived, having marched by a concealed route, and occupying a steep hill between the city and the harbour, shut off from the town the troops who had sallied out. Demetrius, perceiving what had happened, desisted from opposing the landing and collecting his forces and cheering them on started with the intention of fighting a pitched battle with those on the hill. The Romans, seeing the Illyrians advancing resolutely and in good order, formed their ranks and delivered a terrible charge, while at the same time those who had landed from the ships, seeing what was going on, took the enemy in the rear, so that being attacked on all sides the Illyrians were thrown into much tumult and confusion. At the end, being hard pressed both in front and in the rear, Demetrius' troops turned and fled, some escaping to the city, but the greater number dispersing themselves over the island across country. Demetrius had some boats lying ready for such a contingency at a lonely spot, and retreating there and embarking sailed away at nightfall and managed to cross and reach King Philip, at whose court he spent the rest of his life. He was a man of a bold and venturesome spirit, but with an entire lack of reasoning power and judgement, defects which brought him to an end of a piece with the rest of his life. For having, with the approval of Philip, made a foolhardy and ill-managed attempt to seize Messene, he perished in the action, as I shall narrate in detail when we reach that date. Aemilius, the Roman Consul, took Pharos at once by assault and razed it to the ground, and after subduing the rest of Illyria and organizing it as he thought best, returned to Rome late in summer and entered the city in triumph, acclaimed by all, for he seemed to have managed matters not only with ability, but with very high courage.

August 19, Thursday
The Romans hear of the fall of Saguntum

20 The Romans, when the news of the fall of Saguntum reached them, did not assuredly hold a debate on the question of the war, as some authors allege, even setting down the speeches made on both sides — a most absurd proceeding. For how could the Romans, who a year ago had announced to the Carthaginians that their entering the territory of Saguntum would be regarded as a casus belli, now when the city itself had been taken by assault, assemble to debate whether to go to war or not? How is it that on the one hand these authors draw a wonderful picture of the gloomy aspect of the Senate and on the other tell us that fathers brought their sons from the age of twelve upwards to the Senate House, and that these boys attended the debate but divulged not a syllable even to any of their near relatives? Nothing in this is the least true or even probable, unless, indeed, Fortune has bestowed on the Romans among other gifts that of being wise from their cradles. No further criticism, indeed, of such works as those of Chaereas and Sosylus is necessary; they rank in authority, it seems to me, not with history, but with the common gossip of a barber's shop.

September 14, Tuesday
The Romans send ambassadors to Carthage

The Romans, on hearing of the calamity that had befallen Saguntum, at once appointed ambassadors and sent them post-haste to Carthage, giving the Carthaginians the option of two alternatives, the one of which, if they accepted it, entailed disgrace and damage, while the other would give rise to extreme trouble and peril. Either they must give up Hannibal and the members of his Council or war would be declared. On the Roman envoys arriving and appearing before the Senate and delivering their message the Carthaginians listened with indignation to this choice of alternatives, but putting up their most able member to speak, they entered upon their justification.

October 11, Monday
The Second Punic War declared between Carthage and Rome

21 They said not a word of the treaty with Hasdrubal, considering it as not existent, or if existent, as not concerning them, since it was made without their approval. Here they quoted the precedent of the Romans themselves, alleging that the treaty made in the war for Sicily under Lutatius, though agreed to by Lutatius, had been repudiated by the Romans as having been made without their approval. In all their plea of justification they founded and insisted on the treaty at the end of the war for Sicily, in which they said there was no mention of Iberia, but it was expressly set down that the allies of each power should be secure from attack by the other. They pointed out that at that time the Saguntines were not the allies of Rome, and to prove their point they read aloud several extracts from the treaty. The Romans refused definitely to discuss the matter of justification, saying that while Saguntum still stood unharmed matters admitted of a plea of justification and it was possible to reach a decision on the disputed points by argument, but now that the treaty had been broken by the seizure of the city either they must give up the culprits, which would make it clear to all that they had no share in the wrong, but that it had been done without their approval, or if they refused to do so and thus confessed that they were participators in the misdeed they must accept war.

On this occasion the question was dealt with in more or less general terms, but I think it necessary for myself not to neglect it, so that neither those whose duty and interest it is to be accurately informed about this may deviate from the truth in critical debates, nor students, led astray by the ignorance or partisanship of historians, acquire mistaken notions on the subject, but that there may be some survey generally recognized as accurate of the treaties between Rome and Carthage up to our own time.

22 The first treaty between Rome and Carthage dates from the consulship of Lucius Junius Brutus and Marcus Horatius, the first Consuls after the expulsion of the kings, and the founders of the Temple of Jupiter Capitolinus. This is twenty-eight years before the crossing of Xerxes to Greece. I give below as accurate a rendering as I can of this treaty, but the ancient Roman language differs so much from the modern that it can only be partially made out, and that after much application, by the most intelligent men. The treaty is more or less as follows: "There is to be friendship between the Romans and their allies and the Carthaginians and their allies on these terms: The Romans and their allies not to sail with long ships beyond the Fair Promontory unless forced by storm or by enemies: it is forbidden to anyone carried beyond it by force to buy or carry away anything beyond what is required for the repair of his ship or for sacrifice, and he must depart within five days. Men coming to trade may conclude no business except in the presence of a herald or town-clerk, and the price of whatever is sold in the presence of such shall be secured to the vendor by the state, if the sale take place in Libya or Sardinia. If any Roman come to the Carthaginian province in Sicily, he shall enjoy equal rights with the others. The Carthaginians shall do no wrong to the peoples of Ardea, Antium, Laurentium, Circeii, Terracina, or any other city of the Latins who are subject to Rome. Touching the Latins who are not subjects, they shall keep their hands off their cities, and if they take any city shall deliver it up to the Romans undamaged. They shall build no fort in the Latin territory. If they enter the land in arms, they shall not pass a night therein."

23 The "Fair Promontory" is that lying in front of Carthage to the North. The Carthaginians forbid the Romans absolutely to sail south of this on its western side in long ships, the reason being, I think that they did not wish them to become acquainted either with the district round Byssatis or that near the lesser Syrtis, which they call Emporia, owing to their great fertility. If anyone, carried there by a storm or driven by his enemies, requires anything for the purpose of sacrificing to the gods or of repairing his ships, he may have this, but nothing beyond it, and those who touch there must leave within five days. To Carthage itself and all parts of Libya on this side of the Fair Promontory, to Sardinia and the Carthaginian province of Sicily the Romans may come for trading purposes, and the Carthaginian state engages to secure payment of their just debts. The phrasing of this treaty shows that they consider Sardinia and Libya as their own, whereas they distinctly express themselves otherwise about Sicily, mentioning only in the treaty those parts of it which are under Carthaginian rule. Similarly, the Romans include in the treaty Latium alone, making no mention of the rest of Italy as it was not then subject to their authority.

24 At a later date they made another treaty, in which the Carthaginians include Tyre and Utica, and mention, in addition to the Fair Promontory, Mastia and Tarseum as points beyond which the Romans may not either make marauding expeditions, or trade, or found cities. This treaty is more or less as follows: "There is to be friendship on the following conditions between the Romans and their allies and the Carthaginians, Tyrians, and the people of Utica and their respective allies. The Romans shall not maraud or trade or found a city on the farther side of Fair Promontory, Mastia, and Tarseum. If the Carthaginians capture any city in Latium not subject to Rome, they shall keep the valuables and the men, but give up the city. If any Carthaginians take captive any of a people with whom the Romans have a treaty of peace, but who are not subject to Rome, they shall not bring them into Roman harbours, but if one be brought in and a Roman lay hold of him, he shall be set free. The Romans shall not do likewise. If a Roman gets water or provisions from any place over which the Carthaginians rule, he shall not use these provisions to wrong any member of a people with whom the Carthaginians have peace and friendship. The Carthaginians shall not do likewise. If either do so, the aggrieved person shall not take private vengeance, and if he do, his wrongdoing shall be public. No Roman shall trade or found a city in Sardinia and Libya nor remain in a Sardinian or Libyan post longer than is required for taking in provisions or repairing his ship. If he be driven there by stress of weather, he shall depart within five days. In the Carthaginian province of Sicily and at Carthage he may do and sell anything that is permitted to a citizen. A Carthaginian in Rome may do likewise."

Again in this treaty they lay particular stress on Libya and Sardinia, asserting them to be their own private property and closing all landing-places to the Romans, but of Sicily they distinctly speak contrariwise, mentioning the part of it subject to them. Similarly, the Romans in referring to Latium forbid the Carthaginians to wrong the people of Ardea, Antium, Circeii, and Terracina, the cities that stand on the coast of that Latin territory with which the treaty is concerned.

25 A further and final treaty with Carthage was made by the Romans at the time of Pyrrhus' invasion before the Carthaginians had begun the war for Sicily. In this they maintain all the previous agreements and add the following: "If they make an alliance with Pyrrhus, both shall make it an express condition that they may go to the help of each other in whichever country is attacked. No matter which require help, the Carthaginians are to provide the ships for transport and hostilities, but each country shall provide the pay for its own men. The Carthaginians, if necessary, shall come to the help of the Romans by sea too, but no one shall compel the crews to land against their will."

The oaths they had to swear were as follows. In the case of the first treaty the Carthaginians swore by their ancestral gods and the Romans, following an old custom, by Jupiter Lapis, and in the case of this latter treaty by Mars and Quirinus. The oath by Jupiter Lapis is as follows. The man who is swearing to the treaty takes in his hand a stone, and when he has sworn in the name of the state, he says, "If I abide by this my oath may all good be mine, but if I do otherwise in thought or act, let all other men dwell safe in their own countries under their own laws and in possession of their own substance, temples, and tombs, and may I alone be cast forth, even as this stone," and so saying he throws the stone from his hand.

26 The treaties being such, and preserved as they are on bronze tablets beside the temple of Jupiter Capitolinus in the treasury of the Quaestors, who can fail to be surprised at Philinus the historian, not indeed for his ignorance of them, for that is by no means surprising, since still in my time, the most aged among the Romans and Carthaginians and those best versed in public affairs were ignorant of them; but how did he venture and on what authority to state just the opposite, to wit that there was a treaty between Rome and Carthage by which the Romans were obliged to keep away from the whole of Sicily and the Carthaginians from the whole of Italy, and that the Romans broke the treaty and their oath by their first crossing to Sicily? There is, as a fact, no such document at all, nor ever was there; yet in his Second Book he states thus in so many words. I mentioned the subject in the introductory part of this work, but deferred until the present occasion the detailed treatment it deserves, in view of the fact that many people, relying on Philinus' work, have false notions on the subject. True, if as regards the crossing of the Romans to Sicily anyone chooses to blame them for having ever consented to receive into their friendship and afterwards to help those Mamertines who seized treacherously not only Messene but Rhegium, he would have good reason for his disapproval, but if he supposes that they crossed contrary to treaty and to their oath he is obviously ignorant of the true facts.

27 At the close of the war for Sicily, then, they made another treaty, the clauses of which run as follows: "The Carthaginians are to evacuate the whole of Sicily and all the islands between Italy and Sicily. The allies of both parties are to be secure from attack by the other. Neither party is entitled to impose any contribution to construct public buildings, or to enrol soldiers, in the dominions of the other, nor to form alliances with the allies of the other. The Carthaginians are to pay twenty-two hundred talents within ten years, and a sum of a thousand talents at once. The Carthaginians are to give up to the Romans all prisoners free of ransom." Later, at the end of the Libyan War, after the Romans had actually passed a decree declaring war on Carthage, they added the following clauses, as I stated above: "The Carthaginians are to evacuate Sardinia and pay a further sum of twelve hundred talents." The very last of this series of agreements that made with Hasdrubal in Spain, that "The Carthaginians are not to cross the Ebro in arms." Such is the diplomatic history of the relations between Rome and Carthage up to the time of Hannibal.

28 While therefore we find that the crossing of the Romans to Sicily was not contrary to treaty, for the second war, that in which they made the treaty about Sardinia, it is impossible to discover any reasonable pretext or cause. In this case everyone would agree that the Carthaginians, contrary to all justice, and merely because the occasion permitted it, were forced to evacuate Sardinia and pay the additional sum I mentioned. For from the charge brought by the Romans against them in justification of this, that in the Libyan war they inflicted wrongs on the crews of ships sailing from Rome, they had freed them on the occasion when they had received back from them all their sailors who had been brought into Carthage and in return gave back all their own prisoners as an act of grace and without ransom. Of this I have spoken at length in my previous Book.

Having established these facts it remains for us to consider, after thorough investigation, to which of the two states we should attribute the cause of the Hannibalic war.

29 I have already stated what the Carthaginians alleged, and will now give the reply of the Romans — a reply indeed which they did not make at the time owing to their indignation at the loss of Saguntum, but it has been given on many occasions and by many different people at Rome. In the first place they contend that the treaty with Hasdrubal should not be ignored, as the Carthaginians had the audacity to say; for there was no conditioning clause at the end as in the treaty made by Lutatius: "This treaty shall be valid if the Roman people also agree to it," but Hasdrubal finally and unconditionally made the agreement in which was the clause, "The Carthaginians shall not cross the Ebro in arms." Again, in the treaty about Sicily there was, as the Carthaginians admit, the clause: "The allies of either party are to be secure from attack by the other," and this does not mean "those who were allies at that time," as the Carthaginians interpret it; for in that case there would have been a further clause to the effect that neither party should enter into other alliances than their existing ones or that those subsequently received into alliance should not be admitted to the benefits of the treaty. But since neither of these clauses was appended, it is evident that each party undertook that all allies of the other, both those then existing and those subsequently admitted to alliance, should be secure from attack. This indeed seems a quite reasonable view; for surely they would never have made a treaty by which they deprived themselves of the freedom to admit into alliance from time to time any peoples whose friendship seemed to be of advantage to them, nor, having taken such under their protection, was it to be supposed that they would ignore injuries done to them by certain people. But the chief meaning of the treaty to both parties when they made it was, that they should each leave unmolested the existing allies of the other and in no way admit any of those into their own alliance, whereas, regarding subsequent alliances, to which this clause particularly applies, they undertook not to enlist soldiers or levy contributions in the provinces of each or in countries allied to each, and that all allies of each in general should be secure from attack by the other.

30 This being so, it is an acknowledged fact that the Saguntines, a good many years before the time of Hannibal, placed themselves under the protection of Rome. The surest proof of this, and one accepted by the

Carthaginians themselves, is that when a civil disturbance broke out at Saguntum they did not call in the mediation of the Carthaginians, although they were close at hand and already concerning themselves with Spanish matters, but that of the Romans, and with their help set right the affairs of the state. Therefore, if we take the destruction of Saguntum to be the cause of the war we must allow that the Carthaginians were in the wrong in beginning the war, both in view of the treaty of Lutatius, in which it was stipulated that the allies of each should be secure from attack by the other, and in view of the convention made with Hasdrubal, by which the Carthaginians undertook not to cross the Ebro in arms. If, however, we take the cause of the war to have been the robbery of Sardinia and the tribute then exacted, we must certainly confess that they had good reason for entering on the Hannibalic war, since having yielded only to circumstances, they now availed themselves of circumstances to be avenged on those who had injured them.

31 It might be said by some of these who look on such things without discernment, that these are matters which it was not necessary for me to treat in such detail. My answer is, that if there were any man who considered that he had sufficient force in himself to face any circumstances, I should say perhaps that knowledge of the past was good for him, but not necessary; but if there is no one in this world at least who would venture to speak so of himself either as regards his private fortunes or those of his country — since, even if all is well with him now no man of sense could from his present circumstances have any reasonable confidence that he will be prosperous in the future — I affirm for this reason that such knowledge is not only good but in the highest degree necessary. For how can anyone when wronged himself or when his country is wronged find helpmates and allies; how can he, when desirous of acquiring some possession or initiating some project, stir to action those whose co-operation he wishes; how, finally, if he is content with present conditions, can he rightly stimulate others to establish his own convictions and maintain things as they are, if he knows nothing at all of the past history of those he would influence? For all men are given to adapt themselves to the present and assume a character suited to the times, so that from their words and actions it is difficult to judge of the principles of each, and in many cases the truth is quite overcast. But men's past actions, bringing to bear the test of actual fact, indicate truly the principles and opinions of each, and show us where we may look for gratitude, kindness, and help, and where for the reverse. It is by this means that we shall often and in many circumstances find those who will compassionate our distresses, who will share our anger or join us in being avenged on our enemies, all which is most helpful to life both in public and in private. Therefore both writers and readers of history should not pay so much attention to the actual narrative of events, as to what precedes, what accompanies, and what follows each. For if we take from history the discussion of why, how, and wherefore each thing was done, and whether the result was what we should have reasonably expected, what is left is a clever essay but not a lesson, and while pleasing for the moment of no possible benefit for the future.

32 For this reason I must pronounce those to be much mistaken who think that this my work is difficult to acquire and difficult to read owing to the number and length of the Books it contains. How much easier it is to acquire and peruse forty Books, all as it were connected by one thread, and thus to follow clearly events in Italy, Sicily, and Libya from the time of Pyrrhus to the capture of Carthage, and those in the rest of the world from the flight of Cleomenes of Sparta on till the battle of the Romans and Achaeans at the Isthmus, than to read or procure the works of those who treat of particular transactions. Apart from their being many times as long as my history, readers cannot gather anything with certainty from them, firstly because most of them give different accounts of the same matter, and next because they omit those contemporary events by a comparative review and estimation of which we can assign its true value to everything much more surely than by judging from particulars; and, finally, because it is out of their power even to touch on what is most essential. For I maintain that far the most essential part of history is the consideration of the remote or immediate consequences of events and especially that of causes. Thus I regard the war with Antiochus as deriving its origin from that with Philip, the latter as resulting from that with Hannibal, and the Hannibalic war as a consequence of that about Sicily, the intermediate events, however many and various their character, all tending to the same purpose. All this can be recognized and understood from a general history, but not at all from the historians of the wars themselves, such as the war with Perseus or that with Philip, unless indeed anyone reading their descriptions of the battles alone conceives that he has acquired an adequate knowledge of the management and nature of the whole war. This, however, is not at all so, and I consider that my history differs to its advantage as much from the works on particular episodes as learning does from listening.

33 I interrupted my narrative to enter on this digression at the point where the Roman ambassadors were at Carthage. After listening to the Carthaginians' statement of their case, they made no other reply but the following. The oldest member of the embassy, pointing to the bosom of his toga, told the Senate that it held both war and peace for them: therefore he would let fall from it and leave with them whichever of the two they bade him. The Carthaginian Suffete bade him let fall whichever the Romans chose, and when the envoy said he would let fall war, many of the senators cried out at once, "We accept it." The ambassadors and the Senate parted on these terms.

November 03, Wednesday
Sends Iberian troops home for the Winter

Hannibal, who was wintering in New Carthage, in the first place dismissed the Iberians to their own cities hoping thus to make them readily disposed to help in the future;

November 16, Tuesday
Prepares for Alpine journey and readies his brother Hasdrubal to manage Spain in his absence

next he instructed his brother Hasdrubal how to manage the government of Spain and prepare to resist the Romans if he himself happened to be absent; in the third place he took precautions for the security of Africa, adopting the very sensible and wise policy of sending soldiers from Africa to Spain, and vice versa, binding by this measure the two provinces to reciprocal loyalty. The troops who crossed to Africa were supplied by the Thersitae, Mastiani, Iberian Oretes and Olcades, and numbered twelve hundred horse and thirteen thousand eight hundred and seventy Balearians, a popular appellation, derived from ballein, "to throw," and meaning slingers, given to them owing to their skill with this weapon and extended to their nation and islands. He stationed most of these troops at Metagonia in Libya and some in Carthage itself. From the so-called Metagonian towns he sent four thousand foot to Carthage to serve both as a reinforcement and as hostages. In Spain he left with his brother Hasdrubal fifty quinqueremes, two quadriremes and all the triremes being fully manned. He also gave him as cavalry Liby-Phoenicians and Libyans to the number of four hundred and fifty, three hundred Ilergetes and eighteen hundred Numidians drawn from the Masylii, Masaesylii, Maccoei and Maurusi, who dwell by the ocean, and as infantry eleven thousand eight hundred and fifty Libyans, three hundred Ligurians, and five hundred Balearians, as well as twenty-one elephants.

No one need be surprised at the accuracy of the information I give here about Hannibal's arrangements in Spain, an accuracy which even the actual organizer of the details would have some difficulty in attaining, and I need not be condemned off-hand under the idea that I am acting like those authors who try to make their misstatements plausible. The fact is that I found on the Lacinian promontory a bronze tablet on which Hannibal himself had made out these lists during the time he was in Italy, and thinking this an absolutely first-rate authority, decided to follow the document.

34 Hannibal, after taking all precautions for the safety of Africa and Spain, was anxiously awaiting the arrival of the messengers he expected from the Celts. He had informed himself accurately about the fertility of the land at the foot of the Alps and near the river Po, the denseness of its population, the bravery of the men in war, and above all their hatred of Rome ever since that former war with the Romans which I described in the preceding Book to enable my readers to follow all I am about to narrate. He therefore cherished high hopes of them, and was careful to send messengers with unlimited promises to the Celtic chiefs both on this side of the Alps and in the mountains themselves, thinking that the only means of carrying the war against the Romans into Italy was, after surmounting, if possible, the difficulties of the route, to reach the above country and employ the Celts as co-operators and confederates in his enterprise.

218 BC

March 20, Sunday
Reconnaissance that Celts willing to cooperate with Hannibal crossing the Alps

When the messengers arrived and reported that the Celts consented and awaited him, at the same time saying that the crossing of the Alps was very toilsome and difficult, but by no means impossible,

March 29, Tuesday
Troops conveyed from their winter quarters to be trained for his expedition

he drew out his troops from their winter quarters in the early spring.

April 21, Thursday
Rallies his troops

As the news of what had happened in Carthage had just reached him, his spirits were now high, and trusting in the favourable disposition of the citizens,

May 06, Friday
Rallies his troops and continues to train his men

he now called openly on his men to join him in the war against Rome, impressing upon them the demand of the Romans that he and all his principal officers should be given up to them, and pointing out at the same time the wealth of the country they were bound for and the friendly feelings of the Gauls who would be their allies. When he saw that the soldiers listened gladly and were as eager as himself to be off, he commended their alacrity and after ordering them to be ready on the day fixed for his departure, dismissed the meeting.

June 15, Wednesday
Leaves New Carthage and starts campaign for Italy

35 Having completed the arrangements I mentioned above during the winter and thus assured the security of Africa and Spain, he advanced on the day he had fixed with an army of about ninety thousand foot and twelve thousand horse.

July 13, Wednesday
Crosses the Ebro river, likely near the city of Tortosa (the distance between Cartagena and Tortosa is approximately 480km)

Crossing the Ebro,

July 15, Friday
Commences subjugation of local tribes upto the Pyrenees

he set about subduing the tribes of the Ilurgetes, Bargusii, Aerenosii, and Andosini as far as the Pyrenees, and having reduced them all and taken some cities by assault, with unexpected rapidity indeed, but after many severe engagements and with great loss, he left Hanno in command of all the country on this side of the river, placing the Bargusii under his absolute rule, as he mistrusted them most, owing to their friendly sentiments toward Rome. He assigned to Hanno out of his own army ten thousand foot and one thousand horse, and he left with him all the heavy baggage of the expeditionary force. He dismissed at the same time an equal number of troops to their homes, with the view of leaving them well disposed to himself and encouraging the hope of a safe return in the rest of the Spaniards, not only those who were serving with him, but those who remained at home, so that if he ever had to call on them for reinforcements, they might all readily respond. With the rest of his force, thus lightened of its impedimenta and consisting now of fifty thousand foot and about nine thousand horse, he advanced throughout the Pyrenees towards the crossing of the Rhone, having now an army not so strong in number as serviceable and highly trained owing to the unbroken series of wars in Spain.

36 That my narrative may not be altogether obscure to readers owing to their ignorance of the topography I must explain whence Hannibal started, what countries he traversed, and into what part of Italy he descended. Nor must I simply give the names of countries, rivers, and cities, as some authors do under the idea that this is amply sufficient for a clear knowledge. I am of opinion that as regards known countries the mention of names is of no small assistance in recalling them to our memory, but in the case of unknown lands such citation of names is just of as much value as if they were unintelligible and inarticulate sounds. For the mind here has nothing to lean upon for support and cannot connect the words with anything known to it, so that the narrative is associated with nothing in the readers' mind, and therefore meaningless to him. We must therefore make it possible when speaking of unknown places to convey to the reader a more or less real and familiar notion of them.

Now the primary and most general conception and one common to all mankind is the division and ordering of the heavens by which all of us, even those of the meanest capacity, distinguish East, West, South, and North. The next step in knowledge is to classify the parts of the earth under each of these divisions, ever mentally referring each statement to one of them until we arrived at a familiar conception of unknown and unseen regions.

37 This once established as regards the whole earth, it remains for me to lay before my readers the division on the same principle of that portion of the world known to us. This is divided into three parts, each with its name, the one part being called Asia, the second Africa, and the third Europe. Their respective boundaries are the river Don, the Nile, and the straits at the Pillars of Hercules. Asia lies between the Nile and Don and falls under that portion of the heaven lying between the north-east and the south. Africa lies between the Nile and the Pillars of Hercules, and it falls under the south to the south-west and west, as far as the point of the equinoctial sunset, in which latter quarter are the Pillars of Hercules. These two divisions of the earth, then, regarded from a general point of view, occupy the part of it which lies to the south of the Mediterranean, reaching from east to west. Europe lies opposite to them on the north shore of this sea, extending continuously from east to west, its most compact and deepest portion lying due north between the Don and the Narbo, the latter river being not far to the west of Marseilles and of the mouths by which the Rhone discharges itself into the Sardinian Sea. The Celts inhabit the country near the Narbo and beyond it as far as the chain of the Pyrenees which stretches in an unbroken line from the Mediterranean to the Outer Sea. The remaining part of Europe beyond the Pyrenees reaching to its western end and to the Pillars of Hercules is bounded on the one side by the Mediterranean and on the other by the Outer Sea, that portion of which is washed by the Mediterranean as far as the Pillars of Hercules being called Iberia, while that part which lies along the Outer or Great Sea has no general name, as it has only recently come under notice, but is all densely inhabited by barbarous tribes of whom I shall speak more particularly on a subsequent occasion.

38 Just as with regard to Asia and Africa where they meet in Aethiopia no one up to the present has been able to say with certainty whether the southern extension of them is continuous land or is bounded by a sea, so that part of Europe which extends to the north between the Don and Narbo is up to now unknown to us, and will remain so unless the curiosity of explorers lead to some discoveries in the future. We must pronounce that those who either by word of mouth or in writing make rash statements about these regions have no knowledge of them, and invent mere fables.

I have said so much in order that my narrative should not be without something to range itself under in the minds of those who are ignorant of the localities, but that they should have some notion at least of the main geographical distinctions, with which they can connect in thought and to which they can refer my statements, calculating the position of places from the quarter of the heaven under which they lie. For as in the case of physical sight we are in the habit of turning our faces in the direction of any object pointed out to us, so should we mentally ever turn and shift our glance to each place to which the story calls our attention.

39 Dismissing this matter I will now continue my narrative. At the time of which we are speaking the Carthaginians were masters of all that part of Africa which looks towards the Mediterranean from the Altars of Philaenus on the Greater Syrtis as far as the Pillars of Hercules. The length of this coast-line is more than sixteen thousand stades. Crossing the straits at the Pillars of Hercules they had similarly subdued all Iberia as far as the point on the coast of the Mediterranean where the Pyrenees, which separate the Celts from the Iberians, end. This spot is about eight thousand stades distant from the mouth of this sea at the Pillars of Hercules, the distance being three thousand stades from the Pillars to New Carthage, from which place Hannibal started for Italy, two thousand six hundred stades from hence to the Ebro, and from the Ebro to Emporium one thousand six hundred stades. From Emporium to Narbo it is about six hundred stades, and from Narbo to the passage of the Rhone about sixteen hundred, this part of the road having now been carefully measured by the Romans and marked with milestones at every eighth stade. From the passage of the Rhone, following the bank of the river in the direction of its source as far as the foot of the pass across the Alps to Italy, the distance is fourteen hundred stades, and the length of the actual pass which would bring Hannibal down into the plain of the Po, about twelve hundred. So that to arrive there he had, starting from New Carthage, to march about nine thousand stades.

September 06, Tuesday
Arrives at Emporium near modern-day Col du Perthus or Col de Portus at the base of the Pyrenees (this is approximately 340km from Tortosa)

Of this, as far as distance goes, he had nearly traversed the half, but if we look to difficulty far the largest part lay before him.

40 While Hannibal was thus attempting to cross the Pyrenees, in great fear of the Celts owing to the natural strength of the passes, the Romans, having received from the envoys they had sent to Carthage an account of the decision arrived at, and the speeches made there, and on news reaching them sooner than they had expected that Hannibal had crossed the Ebro with his army, determined to send, with their legions, the Consuls Publius Cornelius Scipio to Spain and Tiberius Sempronius Longus to Africa.

While occupied in enrolling the legions and making other preparations they were pushing on the project of establishing in Cisalpine Gaul the colonies on which they had decided. They took active steps to fortify the towns, and ordered the colonists, who were about six thousand in number for either city, to be on the spot within thirty days. The one city they founded on this side of the Po, calling it Placentia, the other, which they named Cremona, on the far side. Scarce had both these colonies been established when the Boii Gauls, who had been for long as it were lying in wait to throw off their allegiance to Rome, but had hitherto found no opportunity, elated now by the messages they received assuring them of the near arrival of the Carthaginians, revolted from Rome, abandoning the hostages they gave at end of the former war which I described in my last Book. Calling on the Insubres to join them, whose support they easily gained owing to their long-standing rancour against Rome, they overran the lands which the Romans had allotted to their colonies and on the settlers taking to flight, pursued them to Mutina, a Roman colony, and there besieged them. Among those shut up there were three men of high rank who had been sent to carry out the partitionment of the country, Gaius Lutatius, a former Consul, and two former Praetors. On these three requesting a parley with the Boii, the latter consented, but when they came out for the purpose they treacherously made them prisoners, hoping by means of them to get back their own hostages. When the Praetor Lucius Manlius, who with his troops was occupying an advanced position in the neighbourhood, heard of this, he hastened up to give help. The Boii had heard of his approach, and posting ambuscades in a certain forest attacked him from all sides at once as soon as he reached the wooded country, and killed many of the Romans. The remainder at first took to flight, but on getting to higher ground rallied just enough to give their retreat an appearance of order. The Boii following at their heels shut this force too up in the place called Vicus Tannetis. When the news reached Rome that the fourth legion was surrounded by the Boii and besieged, they instantly sent off the legions destined for Publius under the command of a Praetor to its assistance, ordering Publius to enrol other legions from the allies.

41 The condition and course of Celtic affairs from the outset up to the arrival of Hannibal were such as I have narrated here and in the previous Book. The two Roman Consuls, having made all preparations for their respective enterprises, set sail early in summer to take in hand the operations determined on, Publius bound for Iberia with sixty ships and Tiberius Sempronius for Africa with a hundred and sixty quinqueremes. With these he threatened such a redoubtable expedition and made such vast preparations at Lilybaeum, collecting all kinds of forces from everywhere, that it seemed as if he expected to sail up to Carthage and at once lay siege to it. Publius, coasting along Liguria, reached the neighbourhood of Marseilles from Pisa in five days, and coming to anchor off the first mouth of the Rhone, known as the Massaliotic mouth, disembarked his forces there, having heard that Hannibal was already crossing the Pyrenees, but convinced that he was still at a distance of many days' march owing to the difficulty of the country and the numbers of Celtic tribes between them. Hannibal, however, who had bribed some of the Celts and forced others to give him passage, unexpectedly appeared with his army at the crossing of the Rhone, having marched with the Sardinian Sea on his right. Publius, when the arrival of the enemy was reported to him, being partly incredulous owing to the cupidity of their advance and partly desirous of ascertaining the exact truth — while he himself was refreshing his troops after their voyage and consulting with his Tribunes in what place it would be wisest to offer battle to the enemy — sent out three hundred of his bravest cavalry, giving them as guides and supports certain Celts who were in the service of the Massaliots as mercenaries.

September 24, Saturday
Arrival near the Rhône river in the vicinity of Avignon

42 Hannibal, on reaching the neighbourhood of the river, at once set about attempting to cross it where the stream is single at a distance of about four days' march from the sea. Doing his best to make friends with the inhabitants of the bank, he bought up all their canoes and boats, amounting to a considerable number, since many of the people on the banks of the Rhone engage in maritime traffic. He also got from them the logs suitable for making the canoes, so that

September 26, Monday
Local inhabitants offer their transportation vehicles

in two days he had an innumerable quantity of ferry-boats, every one doing his best to dispense with any assistance and relying on himself for his chance of getting across. In the meantime a large force of barbarians had gathered on the opposite bank to prevent the Carthaginians from crossing. Hannibal observing this and concluding that as things stood it was neither possible to force a crossing in face of such a strong hostile force nor to put it off, lest he should find himself attacked on all sides, sent off on the third night after his arrival a portion of his army, giving them native guides and placing them under the command of Hanno, the son of Bomilcar the Suffete.

September 28, Wednesday
Advances up the river

Advancing up the bank of the river for two hundred stades they reached a place at which the stream divides, forming an island, and here they stopped.

October 01, Saturday
Construct rafts

Using the timber they found ready to hand and either nailing or lashing logs together they soon constructed a number of rafts sufficient for their present need,

October 02, Sunday
Cross Rhône river

and on these they crossed in safety, meeting with no opposition.

October 03, Monday
Day of rest

Occupying a post of some natural strength they remained there for that day to rest after their exertions and at the same time to prepare for the movement which they had been ordered to execute. Hannibal, moreover, with the part of the army that remained behind with him, was similarly occupied. The question that caused him the greatest embarrassment was how to get the elephants, thirty-seven in number, across.

October 06, Thursday

43 On the fifth night, however, the force which had already crossed began a little before dawn to advance along the opposite bank against the barbarians there, while Hannibal had got his soldiers ready and was waiting till the time for crossing came. He had filled the boats with his light horse and the canoes with his lightest infantry. The large boats were placed highest up stream and the lighter ferry-boats farther down, so that the heavier vessels receiving the chief force of the current the canoes should be less exposed to risk in crossing. They hit on the plan of towing the horses astern of the boats swimming, one man at each side of the stern guiding three or four horses by their leading reins, so that a considerable number were got across at once in the first batch.

October 07, Friday
Battle with the tribes at the Rhône river

The barbarians seeing the enemy's project poured out of their camp, scattered and in no order, feeling sure that they would easily prevent the Carthaginians from landing. Hannibal, as soon as he saw that the force he had previously sent across was near at hand on the opposite bank, they having announced their approach by a smoke-signal as arranged, ordered all in charge of the ferry-boats to embark and push up against the current. He was at once obeyed, and now with the men in the boats shouting as they vied with one another in their efforts and struggled to stem the current, with the two armies standing on either bank at the very brink of the river, the Carthaginians following the progress of the boats with loud cheers and sharing in the fearful suspense, and the barbarians yelling their war-cry and challenging to combat, the scene was in the highest degree striking and thrilling. At this moment, the barbarians having deserted their tents, the Carthaginians on the far bank attacked suddenly and unexpectedly, and while some of them set fire to the enemy's encampment, the larger portion fell upon the defenders of the passage. The barbarians, taken quite by surprise, rushed some of them to save their tents, while others defended themselves against their assailants. Hannibal, all falling out favourably as he had purposed, at once marshalled those of his men who were the first to land, and after addressing some words of exhortation to them, led them to meet the barbarians, upon which the Celts, owing to their disordered condition and to their being taken by surprise, soon turned and took to flight.

44 The Carthaginian general, having thus made himself master of the passage and defeated the enemy, at once occupied himself in fetching over the men who had been left on the other bank, and having in a very short time brought his whole army across encamped for that night beside the river.

October 08, Saturday
Addresses an assembly of his men

Next morning, hearing that the Roman fleet was anchored off the mouths of the Rhone, he selected five hundred of his Numidian horse and sent them off to observe the whereabouts and number of the enemy and what they were about. At the same time he set the proper men to the task of bringing the elephants across and then called a meeting of his soldiers and, introducing Magilus and the other chieftains who had come to him from the plain of the Po, made the troops acquainted through a dragoman with what they reported to be the decision of their tribes. What encouraged the soldiers most in their address was firstly the actual and visible presence of those Gauls who were inviting them to Italy and promising to join them in the war against Rome, and secondly the reliance they placed on their promise to guide them by a route which would take them without their being exposed to any privations, rapidly and safely to Italy. In addition to this the Gauls dwelt on the richness and extent of the country they were going to, and the eager spirit of the men by whose side they were about to face the armies of Rome. The Celts, after speaking in this sense, withdrew, and Hannibal himself now came forward and began by reminding them of their achievements in the past: though, he said, they had undertaken many hazardous enterprises and fought many a battle they had never met with ill success when they followed his plans and counsels. Next he bade them be of good heart considering that the hardest part of their task was now accomplished, since they had forced the passage of the river and had the testimony of their own eyes and ears to the friendly sentiments and readiness to help of their allies. He begged them therefore to be at their ease about details which were his own business, but to obey orders and behave like brave men and in a manner worthy of their own record in the past. When the men applauded him, exhibiting great enthusiasm and ardour, he commended them and, after offering a prayer to the gods on behalf of all, dismissed them, bidding them get everything ready expeditiously as they would start on their march next day.

45 After the assembly had broken up the Numidian scouts who had been sent out to reconnoitre returned, the greater part of the force lost and the remainder in headlong flight. Not far from their own camp they had fallen in with the Roman cavalry sent out by Publius on the same errand, and both forces had shown such heroism in the engagement that the Romans and Celts lost about a hundred and forty horsemen and the Numidians more than two hundred. Afterwards the Romans carried their pursuit close up to the Carthaginian camp, and having surveyed it, turned and hastily rode off to report to the Consul the arrival of the enemy, and on reaching their camp did so. Publius at once put his baggage on board the ships and started with his whole army marching up the river bank with the view of encountering the Carthaginians.

October 09, Sunday
Starts the process of crossing the elephants across the river

Hannibal, on the day after the assembly, advanced his cavalry in the direction of the sea to act as a covering force and then moved his infantry out of the camp and sent them off on their march, while he himself waited for the elephants and the men who had been left with them. The way they got the elephants across was as follows.

46 They built a number of very solid rafts and lashing two of these together fixed them very firmly into the bank of the river, their united width being about fifty feet. To these they attached others on the farther side, prolonging the bridge out into the stream. They secured the side of it which faced the current by cables attached to the trees that grew on the bank, so that the whole structure might remain in place and not be shifted by the current. When they had made the whole bridge or pier of rafts about two hundred feet long they attached to the end of it two particularly compact ones, very firmly fastened to each other, but so connected with the rest that the lashings could easily be cut. They attached to these several towing-lines by which boats were to tow them, not allowing them to be carried down stream, but holding them up against the current, and thus were to convey the elephants which would be in them across. After this they piled up a quantity of earth on all the line of rafts, until the whole was on the same level and of the same appearance as the path on shore leading to the crossing. The animals were always accustomed to obey their mahouts up to the water, but would never enter it on any account, and they now drove them along over the earth with two females in front, whom they obediently followed. As soon as they set foot on the last rafts the ropes which held these fast to the others were cut, and the boats pulling taut, the towing-lines rapidly tugged away from the pile of earth the elephants and the rafts on which they stood. Hereupon the animals becoming very alarmed at first turned round and ran about in all directions, but as they were shut in on all sides by the stream they finally grew afraid and were compelled to keep quiet. In this manner, by continuing to attach two rafts to the end of the structure, they managed to get most of them over on these, but some were so frightened that they threw themselves into the river when half-way across. The mahouts of these were all drowned, but the elephants were saved, for owing to the power and length of their trunks they kept them above the water and breathed through them, at the same time spouting out any water that got into their mouths and so held out, most of them passing through the water on their feet.

October 13, Sunday
Advances up the river bank

47 After the elephants had been put across, Hannibal, taking them and his cavalry and forming these into a rear-guard, advanced up the river bank away from the sea in an easterly direction as though making for the centre of Europe. The Rhone rises north-west of the head of the Adriatic on the northern slope of the Alps, and running in a south-westerly direction, falls into the Sardinian Sea. A great part of its course is through a deep valley, to the north of which lives the Celtic tribe of the Ardyes, while on the south it is bounded for its whole extent by the northern spurs of the Alps. The plain of the Po which I described above at length is separated from the Rhone valley by the lofty main chain of these mountains, which starting from Marseilles extends to the head of the Adriatic. It is this chain which Hannibal now crossed to enter Italy from the Rhone valley.

Some of the writers who have described this passage of the Alps, from the wish to impress their readers by the marvels they recount of these mountains, are betrayed into two vices ever most alien to true history; for they are compelled to make both false statements and statements which contradict each other. While on the one hand introducing Hannibal as a commander of unequalled courage and foresight, they incontestably represent him to us as entirely wanting in prudence, and again, being unable to bring their series of falsehoods to any close or issue they introduce gods and the sons of gods into the sober history of the facts. By representing the Alps as being so steep and rugged that not only horses and troops accompanied by elephants, but even active men on foot would have difficult in passing, and at the same time picturing to us the desolation of the country as being such, that unless some god or hero had met Hannibal and showed him the way, his whole army would have gone astray and perished utterly, they unquestionably fall into both the above vices.

48 For in the first place can we imagine a more imprudent general or a more incompetent leader than Hannibal would have been, if with so large an army under his command and all his hopes of ultimate success resting on it, he did not know the roads and the country, as these writers say, and had absolutely no idea where he was marching or against whom, or in fact if his enterprise were feasible or not? What they would have us believe is that Hannibal, who had met with no check to diminish his high hopes of success, ventured on a course that no general, even after a crushing defeat and utterly at his wits' end, would take, to march, that is, into a country as to which he had no information. Similarly, in what they say about the loneliness, and the extreme steepness and difficulty of the road, the falsehood is manifest. For they never took the trouble to learn that the Celts who live near the Rhone not on one or on two occasions only before Hannibal's arrival but often, and not at any remote date but quite recently, had crossed the Alps with large armies and met the Romans in the field side by side with the Celts who inhabit the plain of the Po (as I narrated in an earlier Book) nor are they aware that there is a considerable population in the Alps themselves; but in entire ignorance of all this they tell us that some hero appeared and showed the road. The natural consequence is that they get into the same difficulties as tragic dramatists all of whom, to bring their dramas to a close, require a deus ex machina, as the data they choose on which to found their plots are false and contrary to reasonable probability. These writers are necessarily in the same spirit and invent apparitions of heroes and gods, since the beginnings on which they build are false and improbable; for how is it possible to finish conformably to reason what has been begun in defiance of it? Of course Hannibal did not act as these writers describe, but conducted his plans with sound practical sense. He had ascertained by careful inquiry the richness of the country into which he proposed to descend and the aversion of the people to the Romans, and for the difficulties of the route he employed as guides and pioneers natives of the country, who were about to take part in his adventure. On these points I can speak with some confidence as I have inquired about the circumstances from men present on the occasion and have personally inspected the country and made the passage of the Alps to learn for myself and see.

49 Now the Roman Consul Publius arrived at the crossing of the river three days after the departure of the Carthaginians, and finding the enemy gone was in the highest degree astonished, as he had been convinced that they would never venture to march on Italy by this route owing to the number and unruly character of the native inhabitants. On seeing that they had done so he returned with all speed to his ships and began to embark his forces. Sending his brother to conduct the campaign in Spain, he himself turned back and made sail for Italy with the design of marching rapidly through Etruria and reaching the foot of the pass over the Alps before the enemy.

October 16, Sunday
Arrival in the land of warring brothers

Hannibal, marching steadily from the crossing-place for four days, reached a place called the "Island," a populous district producing abundance of corn and deriving its name from its situation; for the Rhone and Isère running along each side of it meet at its point. It is similar in size and shape to the Egyptian Delta; only in that case the sea forms the base line uniting the two branches of the Nile, while here the base line is formed by a range of mountains difficult to climb or penetrate, and, one may say, almost inaccessible.

On arriving there he found two brothers disputing the crown and posted over against each other with their armies, and on the elder one making overtures to him and begging him to assist in establishing him on the throne, he consented, it being almost a matter of certainty that under present circumstances this would be of great service to him. Having united with him therefore to attack and expel the other, he derived great assistance from the victor; for not only did he furnish the army with plenty of corn and other provisions but he replaced all their old and worn weapons by new ones, thus freshening up the whole force very opportunely. He also supplied most of them with warm clothing and foot-wear, things of the greatest possible service to them in crossing the mountains. But the most important of all was, that the Carthaginians being not at all easy on the subject of their passage through the territory of the Allobroges, he protected them in the rear with his own forces and enabled them to reach the foot of the pass in safety.

October 21, Friday
Starts ten day march along the Isère river

50 After a ten days' march of eight hundred stades along the bank of the Isère

October 31, Monday
Begins ascent of the Alps

Hannibal began the ascent of the Alps and now found himself involved in very great difficulties. For as long as they had been in flat country, the various chiefs of the Allobroges had left them alone, being afraid both of the cavalry and of the barbarians who were escorting them. But when the latter had set off on their return home, and Hannibal's troops began to advance into the difficult region, the Allobrogian chieftains got together a considerable force and occupied advantageous positions on the road by which the Carthaginians would be obliged to ascend. Had they only kept their project secret, they would have utterly annihilated the Carthaginian army, but, as it was, it was discovered, and though they inflicted a good deal of damage on Hannibal, they did more injury to themselves; for the Carthaginian general having learnt that the barbarians had seized on these critical positions, encamped himself at the foot of the pass, and remaining there sent on in advance some of his Gaulish guides, to reconnoitre and report on the enemy's plan and the whole situation. His orders were executed, and on learning that the enemy remained most strictly at their post during the day-time but retired at night to a neighbouring township, he adapted his measures to this intelligence and arranged the following plan.

November 01, Tuesday

He advanced openly with his whole army, and on approaching the difficult points he encamped not far from the enemy. As soon as it was night, he ordered the fires to be lit, and leaving the greater part of his forces there, took the men most fitted for the enterprise, whom he had lightened of their accoutrements, and passing through the narrow part of the road occupied the posts abandoned by the enemy, who had retired as usual to the town.

November 02, Wednesday
Early-morning battle with the Allobroges in the Alps and rest the remainder of the day

51 At daylight the enemy observed what had happened and at first desisted from their project, but afterwards on seeing the long string of sumpter-animals and horsemen slowly and with difficulty winding up the narrow path, they were tempted by this to molest their march. On their doing so and attacking at several different points, the Carthaginians suffered great loss chiefly in horses and sumpter-mules, not so much at the hands of the barbarians as owing to the ground. For the road up the pass being not only narrow and uneven but precipitous, the least movement or disturbance caused many of the animals to be pushed over the precipice with their packs. It was chiefly the horses on being wounded which caused the disturbance, some of them, terrified by the pain, turning and meeting the pack-animals and others rushing on ahead and pushing aside in the narrow path everything that came in their way, thus creating a general confusion. Hannibal, on seeing this and reflecting that there would be no chance of safety even for those who escaped from the battle if the pack-train were destroyed, took with him the men who had occupied the heights at night and hastened to render assistance to the head of the marching column. He inflicted great loss on the Allobroges, as he was charging from higher ground, but the loss was equally heavy among his own troops, since the column on the march was thrown into further confusion in both directions at once owing to the shouting and struggling of those taking part in this combat. It was only when he had put the greater part of the Allobroges to the sword and compelled the rest to take to flight and run for their own land, that the remainder of the pack-train and the horses got slowly and with great difficulty over the dangerous part, and he himself rallying as many troops as he could after the fight, attacked the town from which the enemy had issued to make their onslaught. He found it nearly deserted, as all the inhabitants had been tempted out by hope of pillage, and seized on it. This proved of great service to him for the future as well as the present; for not only did he recover a number of pack-animals and horses and the men who had been captured together with them, but he got a supply of corn and cattle amply sufficient for two or three days, and in addition to this he struck such terror into the next tribes that none of those in the neighborhood of the ascent were likely to venture to molest him.

52 For the present, he encamped here, and after a stay of one day

November 03, Thursday
Resumes march

resumed his march. For the following days he conducted the army in safety up to a certain point, but

November 06, Sunday
Day four after resuming his march

on the fourth day he was again placed in great danger. The natives near the pass conspired together and came out to meet him with treacherous intentions, holding olive-branches and wreaths, which nearly all the barbarians use as tokens of friendship, just as we Greeks use the herald's staff. Hannibal, who was a little suspicious of such proffer of alliance, took great pains to ascertain what their project and general motives were. When they told him that they knew all about the capture of the city and the destruction of those who had attempted to do him wrong, and assured him that for this reason they were come to him, as they neither wished to inflict nor to suffer any injury, and on their promising to give him hostages from among themselves, he for long hesitated, distrusting their word. But, reflecting that if he accepted their offers, he might perhaps make them more chary of attacking him and more pacific, but that if he refused, they would certainly be his declared enemies, he finally agreed to their proposals, and feigned to accept their friendship. Upon the barbarians now delivering the hostages and providing him with cattle in abundance, and altogether putting themselves unreservedly into his hands, he trusted them in so far as to employ them as guides for the next difficult part of the road.

November 07, Monday
Evening of the march on this day and the one before

But after two days march these same barbarians collecting and following on the heels of the Carthaginians, attacked them as they were traversing a certain difficult and precipitous gorge.

53 On this occasion Hannibal's whole army would have been utterly destroyed, had he not still been a little apprehensive and foreseeing such a contingency placed the pack-train and cavalry at the head of the column and the heavy infantry in the rear. As the latter now acted as a covering force, the disaster was less serious, the infantry meeting the brunt of the attack. But in spite of all this a great many men, pack-animals, and horses were lost. For the enemy being on higher ground skirted along the slopes and either by rolling rocks down or by hurling stones from the hand threw the Carthaginians into such extreme peril and confusion that Hannibal was compelled to pass the night with half his force at a certain place defended by bare rocks and separated from his horses and pack-train, whose advance he waited to cover, until after a whole night's labour they managed to extricate themselves from the defile.

November 08, Tuesday

Next day, the enemy having taken their departure, he joined the cavalry and pack-animals and advanced to the summit of the pass, encountering no longer any massed force of barbarians, but molested from time to time and in certain places by some of them who took advantage of the ground to attack him either from the rear or from the front and carry off some of the pack-animals. In these circumstances the elephants were of the greatest service to him; for the enemy never dared to approach that part of the column in which these animals were, being terrified by the strangeness of their appearance.

November 09, Wednesday
Arrival at the summit in the morning. Nine days of ascent and two days before the setting of the Pleiades in 218 BC. He rested that day and the next. The author suggests this was likely Mt Viso (as Hannibal likely later passed through the nearby Col de la Traversette (see below)

After an ascent of nine days Hannibal reached the summit, and encamping there remained for two days to rest the survivors of his army and wait for stragglers. During this interval a good many of the horses which had broken away in terror and a number of those sumpter-animals which had thrown off their packs returned strangely enough, having followed the track of the march, and came into the camp.

54 As it was now close on the setting of the Pleiads snow had already gathered on the summit, and noticing that the men were in bad spirits owing to all they had suffered up to now and expected to suffer he summoned them to a meeting and attempted to cheer them up, relying chiefly for this purpose on the actual view of Italy, which lies so close under these mountains, that when both are viewed together the Alps stand to the whole of Italy in the relation of a citadel to a city. Showing them, therefore, the plain of the Po, and reminding them of the friendly feelings of the Gauls inhabiting it, while at the same time pointing out the situation of Rome itself, he to some extent restored their spirits.

November 11, Friday
Commences descent from the Alps. The route was likely via Col de la Traversette based on stratigraphic, geochemical and microbiological evidence (please see Mahaney et al. Biostratigraphic Evidence Relating to the Age-old Question of Hannibal's Invasion of Italy, I : History and Geological Reconstruction. Archaeometry 59, 1, 2017, 164–178)

Next day he broke up his camp and began the descent. During this he encountered no enemy, except a few skulking marauders, but owing to the difficulties of the ground and the snow his losses were nearly as heavy as on the ascent. The descending path was very narrow and steep, and as both men and beasts could not tell on what they were treading owing to the snow, all that stepped wide of the path or stumbled were dashed down the precipice. This trial, however, they put up with, being by this time familiar with such sufferings, but they at length reached a place where it was impossible for either the elephants or the pack-animals to pass owing to the extreme narrowness of the path, a previous landslip having carried away about one and a half stades of the face of the mountain and a further landslip having recently occurred, and here the soldiers once more became disheartened and discouraged. The Carthaginian general at first thought of avoiding the difficult part by a detour, but as a fresh fall of snow made progress impossible he had to abandon this project.

55 The state of matters was altogether peculiar and unusual. The new snow which had fallen on the top of the old snow remaining since the previous winter, was itself yielding, both owing to its softness, being a fresh fall, and because it was not yet very deep, but when they had trodden through it and set foot on the congealed snow beneath it, they no longer sunk in it, but slid along it with both feet, as happens to those who walk on ground with a coat of mud on it. But what followed on this was even more trying. As for the men, when, unable to pierce the lower layer of snow, they fell and then tried to help themselves to rise by the support of their knees and hands, they slid along still more rapidly on these, the slope being exceedingly steep. But the animals, when they fell, broke through the lower layer of snow in their efforts to rise, and remained there with their packs as if frozen into it, owing to their weight and the congealed condition of this old snow. Giving up this project, then, Hannibal encamped on the ridge, sweeping it clear of snow, and next set the soldiers to work to build up the path along the cliff, a most toilsome task. In one day he had made a passage sufficiently wide for the pack-train and horses; so he at once took these across and encamping on ground free of snow, sent them out to pasture, and then took the Numidians in relays to work at building up the path,

November 13, Sunday
Elephants brought through the summit

so that with great difficulty in three days he managed to get the elephants across, but in a wretched condition from hunger; for the summits of the Alps and the parts near the tops of the passes are all quite treeless and bare owing to the snow lying there continuously both winter and summer, but the slopes half-way up on both sides are grassy and wooded and on the whole inhabitable.

56 Hannibal having now got all his forces together continued the descent, and

November 15, Tuesday
Arrival at the Italian Plains (fifteen days after he started)

in three days' march from the precipice just described reached flat country. He had lost many of his men by the hands of the enemy in the crossing of rivers and on the march in general, and the precipices and difficulties of the Alps had cost him not only many men, but a far greater number of horses and sumpter-animals. The whole march from New Carthage had taken him five months, and he had spent fifteen days in crossing the Alps, and now, when he thus boldly descended into the plain of the Po and the territory of the Insubres, his surviving forces numbered twelve thousand African and eight thousand Iberian foot, and not more than six thousand horse in all, as he himself states in the inscription on the column at Lacinium relating to the number of his forces.

About the same time, as I stated above, Publius Scipio, leaving his forces with his brother Gnaeus with orders to conduct operations in Spain and vigorously combat Hasdrubal, arrived by sea at Pisa with a small following. Marching through Etruria and taking over from the Praetors the frontier legions which were engaged with the Boii, he reached the plain of the Po, and encamping there, waited for the enemy, being anxious to give him battle.

57 Now that I have brought my narrative and the war the two generals into Italy, desire, before entering upon the struggle, to say a few words on what I think proper to my method in this work. Some readers will perhaps ask themselves why, since most of what I have said relates to Africa and Spain, I have not said a word more about the mouth of the Mediterranean at the Pillars of Hercules, or about the Outer Sea and its peculiarities, or about the British Isles and the method of obtaining tin, and the gold and silver mines in Spain itself, all matters concerning which authors dispute with each other at great length. I have omitted these subjects not because I think they are foreign to my history, but in the first place because I did not wish to be constantly interrupting the narrative and distracting readers from the actual subject, and next because I decided not to make scattered and casual allusions to such matters, but assigning the proper place and time to their special treatment to give as true an account of all as is in my power. No one then need be surprised when in the course of my history I reach such localities, if I avoid for the reason here stated any description of them. But if there be any who insist on such descriptions of each place that may be mentioned, they are perhaps unaware that they are much in the case of gourmands at a supper party who taste everything on the table and neither truly enjoy any dish at the moment nor digest any enough to derive beneficial nourishment from it in the future. So those who act in the same way about reading do not properly attain either present entertainment or future benefit.

58 That no part of history requires more circumspection and more correction by the light of truth than this is evident from many considerations and chiefly from the following. While nearly all authors or at least the greater number have attempted to describe the peculiarities and the situation of the countries at the extremities of the known world, most of them are mistaken on many points. We must therefore by no means pass over the subject, but we must say a word to them, and that not casually and by scattered allusions, but giving due attention to it, and in what we say we must not find fault with or rebuke them, but rather be grateful to them and correct them when wrong, knowing as we do that they too, had they the privilege of living at the present day, would correct and modify many of their own statements. In old times, indeed, we find very few Greeks who attempted to inquire into the outlying parts of the world, owing to the practical impossibility of doing so; for the sea had so many perils that it is difficult to enumerate them, and the land ever so many more. Again, even if anyone by his own choice or by the force of circumstances reached the extremity of the world, that did not mean that he was able to accomplish his purpose. For it was a difficult matter to see many things at all closely with one's own eyes, owing to some of the countries being utterly barbarous and others quite desolate, and it was still more difficult to get information about the things one did see, owing to the difference of the language. Then, even if anyone did see for himself and observe the facts, it was even still more difficult for him to be moderate in his statements, to scorn all talk of marvels and, preferring truth for its own sake, to tell us nothing beyond it.

59 As, therefore, it was almost impossible in old times to give a true account of the regions I speak of, we should not find fault with the writers for their omissions or mistakes, but should praise and admire them, considering the times they lived in, for having ascertained something on the subject and advanced our knowledge. But in our own times since, owing to Alexander's empire in Asia and that of the Romans in other parts of the world, nearly all regions have become approachable by sea or land, since our men of action in Greece are relieved from the ambitions of a military or political career and have therefore ample means for inquiry and study, we ought to be able to arrive at a better knowledge and something more like the truth about lands which were formerly little known. This is what I myself will attempt to do when I find a suitable place in this work for introducing the subject, and I shall then ask those who are curious about such things to give their undivided attention to me, in view of the fact that I underwent the perils of journeys through Africa, Spain, and Gaul, and of voyages on the seas that lie on the farther side of these countries, mostly for this very purpose of correcting the errors of former writers and making those parts of the world also known to the Greeks.

But now returning to the point at which I digressed from my narrative I shall attempt to describe the battles between the Romans and Carthaginians in Italy.

60 I have already stated the strength of Hannibal's army when he entered Italy.

November 16, Wednesday
Encamps at the foot of the Alps

Once arrived there he at first encamped at the very foot of the Alps to refresh his forces. For his men had not only suffered terribly from the toil of ascent and descent of the passes and the roughness of the road but they were also in wretched condition owing to the scarcity of provisions and neglect of their persons, many having fallen into a state of utter despondency from prolonged toil and want of food. For it had been impossible to transport over such ground a plentiful supply of provisions for so many thousand men, and with the loss of the pack-animals the greater part of what they were carrying perished. So that while Hannibal started from the passage of the Rhone with thirty-eight thousand foot and more than eight thousand horse he lost in crossing the passes, as I said above, about half his whole force, while the survivors, owing to the continued hardships they had suffered, had become in their external appearance and general condition more like beasts than men. Hannibal, therefore, made every provision for carefully attending to the men and the horses likewise until they were restored in body and spirit.

November 21, Monday
Attempts creating an alliance with the Taurini

After this, his forces having now picked up their strength, when the Taurini who live at the foot of the mountains quarrelled with the Insubres and showed no confidence in the Carthaginians, he at first made overtures for their friendship and alliance,

November 23, Wednesday
Taurini reject the alliance

but on their rejecting these

November 24, Thursday
Begins siege on the Taurini's chief city

he encamped round their chief city and

November 26, Saturday
Taurini city overcome

reduced it in three days.

November 30, Wednesday
Neighboring tribes submit to Hannibal

By massacring those who had been opposed to him he struck such terror into the neighbouring tribes of barbarians that they all came in at once and submitted to him. The remaining Celtic inhabitants of the plains were impatient to join the Carthaginians, as had been their original design, but as the Roman legions had advanced beyond most of them and cut them off, they kept quiet, some even being compelled to serve with the Romans. Hannibal, in view of this, decided not to delay, but to advance and try by some action to encourage those who wished to take part in his enterprise.

61 Such was the purpose he had in view when the news reached him that Publius had already crossed the Po and was quite near at hand. At first he refused to believe it, reflecting that he had left him only a few days previously near the crossing of the Rhone and that the coasting voyage from Marseilles to Etruria was long and difficult, and learning further by inquiry that the road through Italy from the Tyrrhenian Sea to the Alps was likewise very long and not suited for the march of troops. But when more messengers continued to arrive bringing the same news in a more definite form, he was struck with amazement at the whole project of the Consul and the way he had carried it out. Publius had very much the same feeling; for at first he had never expected that Hannibal would even attempt to cross the Alps with foreign forces, and if he ventured on it he thought that certain destruction awaited them. So that, his anticipations being such, when he heard that Hannibal was safe and was already besieging towns in Italy he was amazed too at his daring and venturesomeness. In Rome itself the intelligence had much the same effect. The stir created by the last news of the Carthaginians — that they had captured Saguntum — had only just subsided, measures had been taken to meet this situation by sending one Consul to Libya who was to besiege Carthage itself, and the other to Spain to fight, as they thought, with Hannibal there; and now news came that Hannibal was in Italy with his army and already laying siege to some cities. The thing therefore seemed altogether astounding to them, and in great alarm they sent urgent orders to Tiberius at Lilybaeum, informing him of the arrival of the enemy and bidding him abandon his present project and hasten to the help of his own country. Tiberius at once collected the crews of his fleet and dispatched it with orders to make for home. From his soldiers he exacted through the Tribunes an oath that they would all be at Ariminum on a certain day before bed-time. This is a city on the Adriatic at the southern edge of the plains of the Po. So that as there was great stir and activity all round, and as the news that arrived was what nobody expected, there was on both sides that intense concern for the future which an enemy cannot afford to neglect.

December 02, Friday
Treatment of the prisoners

62 Hannibal and Publius were now near each other, and they both thought it proper to address their troops in a manner suitable to the occasion. The device by which Hannibal tried to encourage his men was as follows. Mustering the troops, he brought forward certain young men from among the prisoners he had taken molesting his march in the difficult part of the Alpine pass. He had purposely, with a view to the use he was going to make of them, ill-used them: they wore heavy fetters, they had suffered much from hunger, and their bodies were disfigured by the marks of blows. Placing them in the middle of the meeting he exhibited some Gaulish suits of armour, such as their kings are wont to deck themselves with when about to engage in single combat. In addition to these he placed there some horses and had some rich military cloaks brought in. He then asked the young men which of them were willing to do combat with each other, the prizes exhibited being destined for the victor, while the vanquished would be delivered by death from his present misery. When all shouted out with one voice that they were willing to fight, he ordered them to draw lots, and the two on whom the lot fell to arm themselves and do combat. The young men, the moment they heard this, lifted up their hands and prayed to the gods, each eager to be himself one of the chosen. When the result was announced, those on whom the lot had fallen were overjoyed and the rest mournful and dejected, and after the combat was over the remaining prisoners congratulated the fallen champion no less than the victor, as having been set free from many and grievous evils which they themselves were left alive to suffer. The sentiment of most of the Carthaginians was identical; for looking on the misery of the other prisoners as they were led away alive, they pitied them on comparing their fate with that of the dead whom they all pronounced to be fortunate.

63 When Hannibal had by this means produced the disposition he desired in the minds of his troops, he rose and told them that he had brought the prisoners before them designedly in order that clearly seeing in the person of the others what they might themselves have to suffer, they should thence take better counsel at the present crisis. "Fortune," he said, "has brought you to a like pass, she has shut upon in on a like listed field of combat, and the prizes and prospects she offers you are the same. For either you must conquer, or die, or fall alive into the hands of your foes. For you the prize of victory is not to possess horses and cloaks, but to be the most envied of mankind, masters of all the wealth of Rome. The prize of death on the battle-field is to depart from life in the heat of the fight, struggling till your last breath for the noblest of objects and without having learnt to know

THE DIARY OF HANNIBAL BARCA

suffering. But what awaits those of you who are vanquished and for the love of life consent to fly, or who preserve their lives by any other means, is to have every evil and every misfortune for their lot. There is not one of you so dull and unreflecting as to hope to reach his home by flight, when he remembers the length of the road he traversed from his native land, the numbers of the enemies that lie between, and the size of the rivers he crossed. I beg you, therefore, cut off as you are entirely from any such hope, to take the same view of your own situation that you have just expressed regarding that of others. For as you all accounted both the victor and the fallen fortunate and pitied the survivors, so now should you think about yourselves and go all of you to battle resolved to conquer if you can, and if this be impossible, to die. And I implore you not to let the hope of living after defeat enter your minds at all. If you reason and purpose as I urge upon you, it is clear that victory and safety will follow; for none ever who either by necessity or choice formed such a resolve have been deceived in their hope of putting their enemies to flight. And when the enemy have the opposite hope, as is now the case with the Romans, most of them being sure of finding safety in flight as their homes are near at hand, it is evident that the courage of those who despair of safety will carry all before it." The object-lesson and the speech were well received by the troops, in whom they produced the enthusiasm and self-confidence that the speaker desired, and after commending them he dismissed them, ordering them to be ready to start at daybreak.

64 At about the same time date Publius Scipio, who had already crossed the Po and had decided to advance across the Ticinus, ordered those qualified for that task to build a bridge and, summoning a meeting of the rest of his forces, addressed them. Most of what he said related to the exalted position of their country and the achievements of their ancestors; what concerned the present situation was as follows. He said that even if they had had no recent experience of the enemy, the knowledge alone that they were going to fight against Carthaginians should give them unshaken hope of victory. They should regard it as altogether an outrageous and surprising that Carthaginians should dare to face Romans, by whom they had been so often beaten, to whom they had paid so much tribute, and whose slaves almost they had been for so many years. "But now," he went on to say, "when apart from this we can judge more or less by our own experience that these actual men here on the spot do not venture to look us in the face, what should our opinion be as to the future, if we estimate chances correctly? Why! not even their cavalry when they met ours near the Rhone came off well, but after losing many of their number fled disgracefully to their own camp, upon which their general and all his forces, as soon as they knew our soldiers were coming, made a retreat more resembling a flight, and contrary to their original intention chose the route through the Alps from pure fear of us. Hannibal has now arrived," he said, "but he has lost most of his army and the rest are weak and useless owing to hardship; he has lost most of his horses too, and those he has left he has rendered fit for nothing by the length and difficulty of his march." From all this he tried to convince them that they had only to show themselves to the enemy. He bade them above all be encouraged by his own presence, for never would he have abandoned his fleet and the Spanish expedition on which he was dispatched, and made such haste to reach Italy, had it not been evident to him that he was doing a necessary service to his country and that victory was a matter of certainty. When all the troops, owing to the authority of the speaker, and the truth of what he said, showed themselves most ardent for a battle, he commended their alacrity and dismissed them, bidding them hold themselves in readiness to execute his orders.

December 03, Saturday

65 Next day they both advanced along the Po on the bank nearest the Alps, the Romans having the stream on their left and the Carthaginians on their right.

December 04, Sunday

Learning on the following day from their scouts that they were near each other, they both encamped where they were and remained there for the present.

December 05, Monday
Carthaginian and Roman army meet

But next morning both generals took the whole of their cavalry, and Publius his javelineers also, and advanced through the plain with the object of reconnoitring each other's forces. Upon their approaching each other and seeing the clouds of dust they at once got into order for action. Publius, placing his javelineers and the Gaulish cavalry which was with them in front and the rest behind, advanced slowly. Hannibal, putting his bridled cavalry and all the heavier part of it in front, led them to meet the enemy, having his Numidian horse ready on each wing to execute an outflanking movement. Both of the leaders and their cavalry were so anxious to join battle that at the opening of the action the javelineers had no time to discharge their first volley, but gave way at once and retired through the gaps between the troops of their own cavalry, in terror of the impending charge and fearful of being trodden under foot by the horsemen who were bearing down on them. The cavalry met front to front and for some time maintained an evenly balanced contest, the engagement being both a cavalry and infantry one, owing to the number of men who dismounted during its progress. When, however, the Numidians outflanked the Romans and took them in the rear, the javelineers on foot who had at first escaped from the charge of the cavalry were now ridden down by the numbers and force of the Numidians, while the cavalry, who from the outset had been facing the Carthaginians, after suffering heavy loss and inflicting still greater on the enemy, being now attacked by the Numidians also in the rear, broke into flight, most of them scattering in every direction but a few gathering closely round the Consul.

66 Publius now broke up his camp and advanced through the plain to the bridge of the Po, hastening to get his legions across before it was too late. For since the country was all flat, since the enemy was superior in cavalry, and since he himself was severely wounded, he decided to place his forces in safety. Hannibal had at first supposed that the Romans would risk an infantry engagement, but on seeing that they had moved out of their camp, followed them as far as the bridge over the first river, but finding most of the planking from it torn up, but the force set to guard it still remaining at their post by the river side, he took them prisoners to the number of about six hundred, and on hearing that the rest of the Romans were far in advance of him he now wheeled round and marched in the opposite direction up the Po with the object of reaching a place where it was easy to bridge it.

December 07, Wednesday

After two days' march he halted and, constructing a bridge of boats,

December 08, Thursday

ordered Hasdrubal to see to the passage of the army and he himself crossing at once gave a hearing to the envoys who had arrived from the districts round. For immediately upon his success, all the neighbouring Celts hastened, as had been their wish from the outset, to make alliance with the Carthaginians, to provide them with supplies and send them contingents. He received them all courteously, and being now joined by his troops from the opposite bank,

December 09, Friday

he advanced along the Po in the opposite direction to his previous march; for now he marched down stream with the object of encountering the enemy. Meanwhile Publius, having crossed the Po and encamped at Placentia, a Roman colony, where he occupied himself with the cure of himself and the other wounded, and thinking that his forces were now firmly established in a safe position, made no move.

December 10, Saturday
Two days after crossing the river Po

But two days after his crossing Hannibal appeared close at hand and

December 11, Sunday
Two days after crossing the river Po

next day drew up his army in full view of the enemy. Upon their refusing his challenge, he encamped at a distance of about fifty stades from the Roman position.

67 The Celtic contingents in the Roman army, seeing that the prospects of the Carthaginians were now brighter, had come to an understanding with each other, and while all remaining quiet in their tents were waiting for an opportunity to attack the Romans. All in the entrenched camp had had their supper and retired to rest, and

December 12, Monday
Local Celts attack the Romans

the Celts, letting the greater part of the night go by, armed themselves about the morning watch and fell upon the Romans who were encamped nearest to them. They killed or wounded many, and finally, cutting off the heads of the slain,

December 13, Tuesday
Celts visit Hannibal after their victory

went over to the Carthaginians, being in number about two thousand foot and rather less than two hundred horse. They were gladly welcomed on their arrival by Hannibal, who at once, after addressing some words of encouragement to them and promising suitable gifts to all, sent them off to their own cities to announce to their countrymen what they had done and urge them to join him. For he was now quite sure that all would take his part on learning of this act of treachery to the Romans on the part of their own countrymen. When at the same time the Boii came to him and delivered up to him the three Roman officials charged with the partition of their lands, whom, as I mentioned above, they had originally captured by treachery, Hannibal welcomed their friendly advances and made a formal alliance with them through the envoys. He gave the three Romans, however, back to them, advising them to keep them in order through them to get their own hostages back, as had been their original design.

Publius was much concerned at this act of treachery, and taking into consideration that as the Celts had been disaffected for some time, now with this additional incentive all the Gauls round about would go over to the Carthaginians, decided to take precautions for the future. In consequence he broke up his camp that same night a little before daybreak and marched towards the river Trebia and the hills in its neighbourhood, relying on the natural strength of the country and the loyalty of the neighbouring allies.

December 14, Wednesday
Commencement of the chase of Publius

68 Hannibal, on being apprised of their departure, at once sent off his Numidian horse, and shortly afterwards the rest of his cavalry, and himself with his army followed close behind. The Numidians, finding the camp deserted, stopped to set fire to it, which proved of great advantage to the Romans, for had the cavalry at once followed them up and overtaken the baggage-train they would have suffered great loss in the flat country. As it was, most of them succeeded in crossing the Trebia, but those who were left behind in the extreme rear were either cut to pieces or captured by the Carthaginians.

Publius, crossing the Trebia, encamped on the first hills he reached and fortifying his camp with a trench and palisade awaited the arrival of Tiberius and his forces. In the meantime he attended carefully to the treatment of his wound, as he was anxious to be able to take part in the coming battle. Hannibal encamped at a distance of about forty stades from the enemy. The numerous Celtic population of the plain, enthusiastically taking up the cause of the Carthaginians, kept the camp furnished with abundance of provisions and were ready to take their part in any of Hannibal's operations or battles.

December 15, Thursday
Appropriation of Clastidium

When the news of the cavalry engagement reached Rome they were surprised that it had not resulted as they would have expected, but were in no want of pretexts to convince themselves that it was not a defeat, some of them putting down to the Consul's rashness and some to wilful poltroonery on the part of the Celts, assuming this from their subsequent desertion. But on the whole, as their infantry forces were still unimpaired, their trust in final success was likewise undiminished. So that when Tiberius and his legions arrived and marched through the city, the general opinion was that they had only to show themselves to decide the battle. On the soldiers, as they had pledged themselves by oath, assembling at Ariminum, the Consul put himself at their head and advanced with all speed to join Publius. When he had done so he encamped with his own forces near Scipio's, to refresh his men after their forty days' continuous march from Lilybaeum to Ariminum. Meanwhile he made all preparations for a battle and had many close conferences with Scipio, ascertaining the truth about what had occurred, and discussing the present situation with him.

69 At about the same time the town of Clastidium was betrayed to Hannibal by a native of Brundisium, to whom the Romans had entrusted it, the garrison and all the stores of grain falling into his hands. The latter he used for his present needs, but he took the men he had captured with them without doing them any hurt, wishing to make a display of leniency, so that those who were overtaken by adversity would not be terrified and give up hope of their lives being spared by him. He conferred high honours on the traitor, as he was anxious to win over those in positions of authority to the Carthaginian cause.

December 16, Friday
Sends army to raid double-dealing tribes

After this, on observing that some of the Celts who lived between the Trebia and the Po had made alliance with himself, but were negotiating with the Romans also, under the idea that thus they would be safe from both, he dispatched two thousand foot and about a thousand Celtic and Numidian horse with orders to raid their country. On his orders being executed and

December 17, Saturday
Carthaginians win large booty

a large amount of booty secured, the Celts at once came into the Roman camp asking for help.

December 18, Sunday
Skirmish between Tiberius and the Carthaginians

Tiberius had long been on the look-out for some ground justifying an active step and now that he had this pretext sent out the greater part of his cavalry and about a thousand javelineers on foot. Making all dispatch they met the enemy beyond the Trebia and on their disputing possession of the booty with them the Celts and Numidians gave way and began to retire on their own camp. Those in command of the advanced posts outside the Carthaginian camp soon understood what had happened and sent out a covering force to support the fugitives, upon which the Romans in their turn were put to flight and fell back on their camp. Tiberius on seeing this ordered out all his remaining cavalry and javelineers, and when these had joined the rest, the Celts again gave way and retreated to a position of safety. The Carthaginian general, as he was not at this time prepared for a general battle, and took the view that a decisive engagement should never be undertaken on any chance pretext and without a definite purpose — as we must pronounce to be the part of a good general — made the men in retreat halt and face about when they approached the camp, but he would not allow them to advance and engage the enemy, calling them back by his officers and buglers. The Romans after waiting for a short time retired after losing a few of their own number, but inflicting a larger loss on the Carthaginians.

70 Tiberius, elated and overjoyed by his success, was all eagerness to bring on a decisive battle as soon as possible. He was, it is true, at liberty to act as he thought best owing to the illness of Scipio, but wishing to have his colleague's opinion he spoke to him on the subject. Scipio's view of the situation was just the opposite. He considered that their legions would be all the better for a winter's drilling, and that the notoriously fickle Celts would not remain loyal to the Carthaginians if the latter were kept in forced inaction, but would throw them over in their turn. Besides he hoped himself when his wound was healed to be of some real service in their joint action. On all these grounds therefore he advised Tiberius to let matters remain where they were. Tiberius was quite conscious of the truth and cogency of all these reasons, but, urged on by his ambition and with an unreasonable confidence in his fortune, he was eager to deliver the decisive blow himself and did not wish Publius to be able to be present at the battle, or that the Consuls designate should enter upon office before all was over — it being now nearly the time for this. Since, then, he did not choose the time indicated by circumstances, but his own time, his action was bound to be mistaken.

Hannibal's view of the situation was very much the same as Scipio's; so that he on the other hand was anxious to force a battle on the enemy, wishing in the first place to avail himself of the enthusiasm of the Celts while still fresh, secondly to encounter the Roman legions while still newly-levied and undrilled, thirdly to fight the battle before Scipio had recovered, but most of all to be up and doing and not let the time slip away resultlessly. For when a general has brought his army into a foreign country and is engaged in such a risky enterprise, his only hope of safety lies in constantly keeping alive the hopes of his allies.

Such, then, was the purpose of Hannibal, who knew that Tiberius was sure to be aggressively inclined.

December 19, Monday
Plan of ambush

71 He had long ago noticed a place between the two camps, flat indeed and treeless, but well adapted for an ambuscade, as it was traversed by a water-course with steep banks densely overgrown with brambles and other thorny plants, and here he proposed to lay a stratagem to surprise the enemy. It was probable that he would easily elude their vigilance; for the Romans, while very suspicious of thickly-wooded ground, which the Celts usually chose for their ambuscades, were not at all afraid of flat and treeless places, not being aware that they are better adapted than woods for the concealment and security of an ambush, because the men can see all round them for a long distance and have at the same time sufficient cover in most cases. Any water-course with a slight bank and reeds or bracken or some kind of thorny plants can be made use of to conceal not only infantry, but even the dismounted horsemen at times, if a little care be taken to lay shields with conspicuous devices inside uppermost on the ground and hide the helmets under them.

The Carthaginian general now consulted with his brother Mago and the rest of the staff about the coming battle, and on their all approving of his plan, after the troops had had their supper, he summoned Mago, who was still quite young, but full of martial enthusiasm and trained from boyhood in the art of war, and put under his command a hundred men from the cavalry and the same number of infantry. During the day he had ordered these men, whom he had marked as the most stout-hearted in his army, to come to his tent after supper. After addressing them and working up their zeal to the required pitch, he ordered each of them to pick out ten of the bravest men from his own company and to come to a certain place in the camp known to them. They did as they were bidden and in the night he sent out the whole force, which now amounted to a thousand horse and as many foot, to the ambuscade, furnishing them with guides and giving his brother orders about the time to attack.

December 20, Tuesday
Battle of Trebia (Winter Solstice)

At daybreak he mustered his Numidian horsemen, all men capable of great endurance, whom he ordered, after having addressed them and promised certain gifts to those who distinguished themselves, to ride up to the enemy's camp, and crossing the river with all speed to draw out the Romans by shooting at them, his wish being to get the enemy to fight him before they had breakfasted or made any preparations. He then collected the other officers and exhorted them likewise to battle, and he ordered the whole army to get their breakfasts and to see to their arms and horses.

72 Tiberius, when he saw the Numidian horse approaching, sent out at first only his cavalry with orders to close with the enemy. He next dispatched about six thousand javelineers on foot and then began to move his whole army out of the camp, thinking that the mere sight of them would decide the issue, so much confidence did his superiority in numbers and the success of his cavalry on the previous day give him. The time of year was about the winter solstice, and the day exceedingly cold and snowy, while the men and horses nearly all left the camp without having had their morning meal. At first their enthusiasm and eagerness sustained them, but when they had to cross the Trebia, swollen as it was owing to the rain that had fallen during the night higher up the valley than where the armies were, the infantry had great difficulty in crossing, as the water was breast-high. The consequence was that the whole force suffered much from cold and also from hunger, as the day was now advancing. The Carthaginians, on the contrary, who had eaten and drunk in their tents and looked after their horses, were all anointing and arming themselves around their fires. Hannibal, who was waiting for his opportunity, when he saw that the Romans had crossed the river, threw forward as a covering force his pikemen and slingers about eight thousand in number and led out his army. After advancing for about eight stades he drew up his infantry, about twenty thousand in number, and consisting of Spaniards, Celts, and Africans, in a single line, while he divided his cavalry, numbering, together with the Celtic allies, more than ten thousand, and stationed them on each wing, dividing also his elephants and placing them in front of the wings so that his flanks were doubly protected. Tiberius now recalled his cavalry, perceiving that they could not cope with the enemy, as the Numidians easily scattered and retreated, but afterwards wheeled round and attacked with great daring — these being their peculiar tactics. He drew up his infantry in the usual Roman order. They numbered about sixteen thousand Romans and twenty thousand allies, this being the strength of their complete army for decisive operations, when the Consuls chance to be united. Afterwards placing his cavalry, numbering about four thousand, on each wing he advanced on the enemy in imposing style marching in order at a slow step.

73 When they were nearly at close quarters, the light-armed troops in the van of each army began the combat, and here the Romans laboured under many disadvantages, the efficiency of the Carthaginians being much superior, since the Roman javelineers had had a hard time since daybreak, and had spent most of their missiles in the skirmish with the Numidians, while those they had left had been rendered useless by the continued wet weather. The cavalry and the whole army were in much the same state, whereas just the opposite was the case with the Carthaginians, who, standing in their ranks fresh and in first-rate condition, were ready to give efficient support wherever it was required. So when the skirmishers had retired through the gaps in their line and the heavy-armed infantry met, the Carthaginian cavalry at once pressed on both flanks of the enemy, being greatly superior in numbers and the condition of themselves and their horses, having, as I explained above, started quite fresh. When the Roman cavalry fell back and left the flanks of the infantry exposed, the Carthaginian pike-men and the Numidians in a body, dashing past their own troops that were in front of them, fell on the Romans from both flanks, damaging them severely and preventing them from dealing with the enemy in their front. The heavy-armed troops on both sides, who occupied the advanced centre of the whole formation, maintained for long a hand-to-hand combat with no advantage on either side.

74 But now the Numidians issued from their ambuscade and suddenly attacked the enemy's centre from the rear, upon which the whole Roman army was thrown into the utmost confusion and distress. At length both of Tiberius' wings, hard pressed in front by the elephants and all round their flanks by the light-armed troops, turned and were driven by their pursuers back on the river behind them. After this, while the rear of the Roman centre was suffering heavy loss from the attack of the ambuscade, those in the van, thus forced to advance, defeated the Celts and part of the Africans, and after killing many of them broke through the Carthaginian line. But seeing that both their flanks had been forced off the field, they despaired of giving help there and of returning to their camp, afraid as they were of the very numerous cavalry and hindered by the river and the force and heaviness of the rain which was pouring down on their heads. They kept, however, in close order and retired on Placentia, being not less than ten thousand in number. Of the remainder the greater part were killed near the river by the elephants and cavalry, but the few infantry who escaped and most of the cavalry retreated to join the body I just mentioned and with them got safely into Placentia. The Carthaginian army, after pursuing the enemy as far as the river, being unable to advance further owing to the storm, returned to their camp. They were all highly elated at the result of the battle, regarding it as a signal success; for very few Africans and Spaniards had been killed, the chief loss having fallen on the Celts. They suffered so severely, however, from the rain and the snow that followed that all the elephants perished except one, and many men and horses also died of the cold.

December 21, Wednesday
Day after the Battle of Trebia

75 Tiberius, though well knowing the facts, wished as far as possible to conceal them from those in Rome, and therefore sent messengers to announce that a battle had taken place and that the storm had deprived him of the victory. The Romans at first gave credence to this news, but when shortly afterwards they learnt that the Carthaginians still kept their camp and that all the Celts had gone over to them, but that their own forces had abandoned their camp and retreated from the field and were now all collected in cities, and getting their supplies up from the sea by the river Po, they quite realized what had been the result of the battle. Therefore, although they were much taken by surprise, they adopted all manner of steps to prepare for the war and especially to protect exposed points, dispatching legions to Sardinia and Sicily and sending garrisons to Tarentum and other suitable places, and getting ready also a fleet of sixty quinqueremes. Gnaeus Servilius and Gaius Flaminius, the Consuls designate, were busy mustering the allies and enrolling their own legions, sending depots of supplies at the same time to Ariminum and Etruria which they meant to be their bases in the campaign. They also applied for help to Hiero, who sent them five hundred Cretans and a thousand light infantry, and on all sides they made active preparations. For the Romans both in public and in private are most to be feared when they stand in real danger.

76 During this time Gnaeus Cornelius Scipio, who, as I said, had been left by his brother Publius in command of the naval forces, sailing from the mouths of the Rhone with his whole fleet to the place in Spain called Emporium, and starting from there made a series of landings, reducing by siege the towns on the coast as far as the Ebro, which refused his advances, but bestowing favours on those which accepted them and taking all possible precautions for their safety. After securing all the sea-board places which had submitted to him he advanced with his whole army into the interior, having now got together also a considerable force of Iberian allies. He won over some of the towns on the line of his march and subdued others, and when the Carthaginians who had been left to guard this district under the command of Hanno encamped opposite to him near a city called Cissa, Gnaeus defeated them in a pitched battle, possessing himself of a large amount of valuable booty — all the heavy baggage of the army that had set out for Italy having been left under their charge — securing the alliance of all the tribes north of the Ebro and taking prisoners the Carthaginian general Hanno and the Iberian general Andobales. The latter was despot of all central Iberia and a strenuous supporter of the Carthaginians. Hasdrubal soon got news of the disaster and crossing the Ebro came to the rescue. Learning that the crews of the Roman ships had been left behind and were off their guard and unduly confident owing to the success of the land forces, he took with him about eight thousand infantry and a thousand cavalry from his own force, and finding the men from the ships scattered over the country, killed a large number of them and compelled the remainder to take refuge on board their vessels. He then retreated, and recrossing the Ebro busied himself with fortifying and garrisoning the places south of the Ebro, passing the winter in New Carthage. Gnaeus, on rejoining the fleet, inflicted the customary penalty on those responsible for what had happened, and now uniting his land and sea forces went into winter quarters at Tarraco. By dividing the booty in equal shares among his soldiers he made them very well disposed to him and ready to do their best in the future.

217 BC (LEAP YEAR)

January-April
Winter rest in Northern Italy at Cisalpine Gaul (likely in the region of modern Ferrara)

77 Such was the state of matters in Spain. In the early spring Gaius Flaminius with his army advanced through Etruria and encamped before Arretium, while Gnaeus Servilius advanced as far as Ariminum to watch for the invasion of the enemy from that side. Hannibal, who was wintering in Cisalpine Gaul, kept the Roman prisoners he had taken in the battle in custody, giving them just sufficient to eat, but to the prisoners from the allies he continued to show the greatest kindness, and afterwards called a meeting of them and addressed them, saying that he had not come to make war on them, but on the Romans for their sakes and therefore if they were wise they should embrace his friendship, for he had come first of all to re-establish the liberty of the peoples of Italy and also to help them to recover the cities and territories of which the Romans had deprived them. Having spoken so, he dismissed them all to their homes without ransom, his aim in doing so being both to gain over the inhabitants of Italy to his own cause and to alienate their affections from Rome, provoking at the same time to revolt those who thought their cities or harbours had suffered damage by Roman rule.

78 During this winter he also adopted a truly Punic artifice. Fearing the fickleness of the Celts and possible attempts on his life, owing to his establishment of the friendly relations with them being so very recent, he had a number of wigs made, dyed to suit the appearance of persons differing widely in age, and kept constantly changing them, at the same time also dressing in a style that suited the wig, so that not only those who had seen him but for a moment, but even his familiars found difficulty in recognizing him.

Observing that the Celts were dissatisfied at the prosecution of the war in their own territory, but were eagerly looking forward to an invasion of that of the enemy, professedly owing to their hatred of the Romans, but as a fact chiefly in hope of booty, he decided to be on the move as soon as possible and satisfy the desire of his troops. As soon, then, as the weather began to change he ascertained by inquiring from those who knew the country best that the other routes for invading the Roman territory were both long and obvious to the enemy, but that the road through the marshes to Etruria was difficult indeed but expeditious and calculated to take Flaminius by surprise. As he was by nature always inclined to such expedients, he decided to march by this road. When the news spread in the camp that the general was going to lead them through marshes, everyone was very reluctant to start, imagining that there would be deep bogs and quagmires.

May 11, Friday
Commences campaign in spring

79 But Hannibal had made careful inquiries, and having ascertained that the water on the ground would have to pass over was shallow and the bottom solid, broke up his quarters and started, placing in the van the Africans and Spaniards and all the most serviceable portion of his army, intermingling the baggage train with them, so that for the present they might be kept supplied with food. For as regards the future he did not trouble himself about the pack-animals at all, as he calculated that on reaching the enemy's country he would, if defeated, have no need of provisions, and if he gained command of the open country would be in no want of supplies. Behind the troops I mentioned he placed the Celts and in the extreme rear his cavalry, leaving his brother Mago in charge of the rear-guard. This course he took for various reasons, but chiefly owing to the softness and aversion to labour of the Celts, so that if, owing to the hardships they suffered, they tried to turn back Mago could prevent them by falling on them with his cavalry.

May 19, Saturday
Arrival at North Italian marshes (likely just outside Ravenna) approximately 70km from Ferrara

The Spaniards and Africans for their part, as the marshes were still firm when they marched over them, got across without suffering seriously, being all inured to fatigue and accustomed to such hardships, but the Celts not only progressed with difficulty, the marshes being now cut up and trodden down to some depth, but were much fatigued and distressed by the severity of the task, being quite unused to suffering of the kind. They were prevented, however, from turning back by the cavalry in their rear.

May 22, Tuesday
Suffers eye infection and encamps just outside Arretium (modern-day Rimini)

All the army, indeed, suffered much, and chiefly from want of sleep, as they had to march through water for three continuous days and nights, but the Celts were much more worn out and lost more men than the rest. Most of the pack-animals fell and perished in the mud, the only service they rendered being that when they fell the men piled the packs on their bodies and lay upon them, being thus out of the water and enabled to snatch a little sleep during the night. Many of the horses also lost their hooves by the continuous march through the mud. Hannibal himself on the sole remaining elephant got across with much difficulty and suffering, being in great pain from a severe attack of ophthalmia, which finally led to the loss of one eye as he had no time to stop and apply any treatment to it, the circumstances rendering that impossible.

80 Having thus almost beyond expectation crossed the marshes, and, finding that Flaminius was encamped in Etruria before the city of Arretium, he pitched his camp for the present at the edge of the marshes, with the view of refreshing his forces and getting information about the enemy and about the country in front of him. On learning that this country promised a rich booty, and that Flaminius was a thorough mob-courtier and demagogue, with no talent for the practical conduct of war and exceedingly self-confident withal, he calculated that if he passed by the Roman army and advanced into the country in his front, the Consul would on the one hand never look on while he laid it waste for fear of being jeered at by his soldiery; and on the other hand he would be so grieved that he would be ready to follow anywhere, in his anxiety to gain the coming victory himself without waiting for the arrival of his colleague. From all this he concluded that Flaminius would give him plenty of opportunities of attacking him.

81 And all this reasoning on his part was very wise and sound. For there is no denying that he who thinks that there is anything more essential to a general than the knowledge of his opponent's principles and character, is both ignorant and foolish. For as in combats between man and man and rank and rank, he who means to conquer must observe how best to attain his aim, and what naked or unprotected part of the enemy is visible, so he who is in command must try to see in the enemy's general not what part of his body is exposed, but what are the weak spots that can be discovered in his mind. For there are many men who, owing to indolence and general inactivity, bring to utter ruin not only the welfare of the state but their private fortunes as well; while there are many others so fond of wine that they cannot even go to sleep without fuddling themselves with drink; and some, owing to their abandonment to venery and the consequent derangement of their minds, have not only ruined their countries their fortunes but brought their lives to a shameful end. But cowardice and stupidity are vices which, disgraceful as they are in private to those who have them, are when found in a general the greatest of public calamities. For not only do they render his army inefficient but often expose those who confide in him to the greatest perils. Rashness on the other hand on his part and undue boldness and blind anger, as well as vaingloriousness and conceit, are easy to be taken advantage of by his enemy and are most dangerous to his friends; for such a general is the easy victim of all manner of plots, ambushes, and cheatery. Therefore the leader who will soonest gain a decisive victory, is he who is able to perceive the faults of others, and to choose that manner and means of attacking the enemy which will take full advantage of the weaknesses of their commander. For just as a ship if deprived of its pilot will fall with its whole crew into the hands of the enemy, so the general who is his opponent's master in strategy and reasoning may often capture his whole army.

And in this case too, as Hannibal had correctly foreseen and reckoned on the conduct of Flaminius, his plan had the success he expected.

May 26, Saturday
Travels beyond the Roman camp

82 For as soon as he left the neighbourhood of Faesulae and advancing a short way beyond the Roman camp invaded the country in front of him,

May 28, Monday
Flaminius begins to lays waste to the countryside

Flaminius swelled with fury and resentment, thinking that the enemy were treating him with contempt. And when very soon they began to lay waste the country, and the smoke rising from all quarters told its tale of destruction, he was still more indignant, regarding this as insufferable. So that when some of his officers gave it as their opinion that he should not instantly pursue and engage the enemy, but remain on his guard and beware of their numerous cavalry, and when they especially urged him to wait until his colleague joined him and to give battle with all their united legions, he not only paid no attention to the advice, but could not listen with patience to those who offered it, begging them to consider what would be said in Rome if, while the country was laid waste almost up to the walls, the army remained encamped in Etruria in the rear of the enemy. Finally, with these words, he broke up the camp, and advanced with his army, utterly regardless of time or place, but bent only on falling in with the enemy, as if victory were a dead certainty. He had even inspired the people with such confident hopes that the soldiery were outnumbered by the rabble that followed him for the sake of the booty, bringing chains, fetters, and other such implements.

June 07, Thursday
The distance between Rimini and Trasimene is approximately 110km

Hannibal in the meantime while advancing on Rome through Etruria, with the city of Cortona and its hills on the left and the Thrasymene lake on his right, continued to burn and devastate the country on his way, with the view of provoking the enemy. When he saw Flaminius already approaching him and had also observed a position favourable for his purpose, he made his plans for battle.

June 11, Monday

83 The road led through a narrow strip of level ground with a range of high hills on each side of it lengthwise. This defile was overlooked in front crosswise by a steep hill difficult to climb, and behind it lay the lake, between which and the hill side the passage giving access to the defile was quite narrow. Hannibal coasting the lake and passing through the defile occupied himself the hill in front, encamping on it with his Spaniards and Africans; his slingers and pikemen he brought round to the front by a detour and stationed them in an extended line under the hills to the right of the defile, and similarly taking his cavalry and the Celts round the hills on the left he placed them in a continuous line under these hills, so that the last of them were just at the entrance to the defile, lying between the hillside and the lake.

June 16, Saturday

Having made all these preparations during the night and thus encompassed the defile with troops waiting in ambush, Hannibal remained quiet. Flaminius was following close on his steps impatient to overtake him. He had encamped the night before at a very late hour close to the lake itself; and

June 17, Sunday
Battle of Lake Trasimene (corroboration with multiple ancient calendars by Chris Bennet at http://www.tyndalehouse.com/Egypt/ptolemies/chron/roman/217 bc.htm)

next day as soon as it was dawn he led his vanguard along the lake to the above-mentioned defile, with the view of coming in touch with the enemy.

84 It was an unusually misty morning, and Hannibal, as soon as the greater part of the enemy's column had entered the defile and when the head was already in contact with him, giving the signal for battle and sending notice to those in the ambuscades, attacked the Romans from all sides at the same time. The sudden appearance of the enemy took Flaminius completely by surprise, and as the condition of the atmosphere rendered it very difficult to see, and their foes were charging down on them in so many places from higher ground, the Roman Centurions and Tribunes were not only unable to take any effectual measures to set things right, but could not even understand what was happening. They were charged at one and the same instant from the front, from the rear, and from the flanks, so that most of them were cut to pieces in marching order as they were quite unable to protect themselves, and, as it were, betrayed by their commander's lack of judgement. For while they were still occupied in considering what was best to do, they were being slaughtered without realizing how. Flaminius himself, who was in the utmost dismay and dejection, was here attacked and slain by certain Celts. So there fell in the valley about fifteen thousand of the Romans, unable either to yield to circumstances, or to achieve anything, but deeming it, as they had been brought up to do, their supreme duty not to fly or quit their ranks. Those again who had been shut in between the hillside and the lake perished in a shameful and still more pitiable manner. For when they were forced into the lake in a mass, some of them quite lost their wits and trying to swim in their armour were drowned, but the greater number, wading into the lake as far as they could, stood there with only their heads out of the water, and when the cavalry approached them, and death stared them in the face, though lifting up their hands and entreating to be spared in the most piteous terms, they were finally dispatched either by the horsemen or in some cases by begging their comrades to do them this service. About six thousand of those in the defile, who had defeated the enemy in their front, were unable to render any assistance to their own army or to get to the rear of their adversaries, as they could see nothing of what was happening, although they might have been of very material service. They simply continued to press forward in the belief that they were sure to meet with someone until they found themselves isolated on the high ground and on reaching the crest of the hill, the mist having now broken, they perceived the extent of the disaster, but were no longer able to help, as the enemy were now completely victorious and in occupation of all the ground. They therefore retired in a body to a certain Etruscan village. After the battle, on Maharbal being sent by the general with the Spaniards and pikemen to surround the village, finding themselves beset by a complication of dangers they laid down their arms and surrendered on condition of their lives being spared.

Such was the result of the battle in Etruria between the Romans and Carthaginians.

June 18, Monday
Day after the Battle of Lake Trasimene

85 Hannibal, when the prisoners who had surrendered on terms as well as the others were brought to him, assembled the whole body, more than fifteen thousand in number, and after informing them in the first place that Maharbal had no authority without consulting him to promise the former their safety, launched out into an invective the Romans, and at the end of it distributed such of the prisoners as were Romans among his troops to keep guard over, and setting all the allies free, sent them to their homes, adding, as on a previous occasion, that he was not come to fight with the Italians, but with the Romans for the freedom of Italy. He now allowed his own troops to rest and paid the last honours to those of the highest rank among the fallen, about thirty in number, his whole loss having been about fifteen hundred, most of them Celts. After this he consulted with his brother and friends as to where and how it was best to deliver his attack, being now quite confident of final success.

June 19, Tuesday
News of the defeat in Rome

On the news of the defeat reaching Rome the chiefs of the state were
unable to conceal or soften down the facts, owing to the magnitude of the
calamity, and were obliged to summon a meeting of the commons and
announce it. When the Praetor therefore from the Rostra said, "We have
been defeated in a great battle," it produced such consternation that to
those who were present on both occasions the disaster seemed much
greater now than during the actual battle. And this was quite natural; for
since for many years they had had no experience of the word or fact of
avowed defeat, they could not bear the reverse with moderation and dignity.
This was not, however, the case with the Senate, which remained self-
possessed, taking thought for the future as to what should be done by
everyone, and how best to do it.

86 At the time of the battle Gnaeus Servilius, the Consul in command in
the district of Ariminum (the district that is on the coast of the Adriatic
where the plain of Cisalpine Gaul joins the rest of Italy not far from the
mouth of the river Po), hearing that Hannibal had invaded Etruria and was
encamped opposite Flaminius, formed the project of joining the latter with
his whole army, but as this was impossible owing to the weight of his forces
he dispatched Gaius Cenetenius at once in advance, giving him four
thousand horse, intending them, if the situation were critical, to press on
and arrive before himself.

June 20, Wednesday
News of Roman reinforcement force on the charge

When, after the battle, news reached Hannibal of the approach of these
reinforcements,

June 21, Thursday
Roman reinforcements defeated

he sent off Maharbal with the pikemen and part of the cavalry.
Encountering Gaius, they killed about half of his force in their first attack,
and pursuing the others to a hill, made them all prisoners on the following
day.

June 22, Friday
News of the second successive defeat in Rome

Three days after the news of the great battle had reached Rome, and just when throughout the city the sore, so to speak, was most violently inflamed, came the tidings of this fresh disaster, and now not only the populace but the Senate too were thrown into consternation. Abandoning therefore the system of government by magistrates elected annually they decided to deal with the present situation more radically, thinking that the state of affairs and the impending peril demanded the appointment of a single general with full powers.

June 25, Monday
Begins travel through the Italian countryside toward the Adriatic coast

Hannibal, now fully assured of success, dismissed the idea of approaching Rome for the present, but began to ravage the country unmolested, advancing towards the Adriatic.

July 05, Thursday
Arrives at the Adriatic coast (near modern-day Pesaro)

Passing through Umbria and Picenum he reached the coast on the tenth day, having possessed himself of so large an amount that his army could not drive or carry it all off and having killed a number of people on his road. For, as at the capture of cities by assault, the order had been given to put to the sword all adults who fell into their hands, Hannibal acting thus owing to his inveterate hatred of the Romans.

87 He now encamped near the Adriatic in a country abounding in all kinds of produce, and paid great attention to recruiting the health of his men as well as his horses by proper treatment. In consequence of the cold from which they had sufficient while wintering in the open land of Gaul, combined with their being unable to get the friction with oil to which they were accustomed, and owing also to the hardships of the subsequent march through the marshes, nearly all the horses as well as the men had been attacked by so-called "hunger-mange" and its evil results. So that, now he was in occupation of such a rich country, he built up his horses and restored the physical and mental condition of his men. He also re-armed the Africans in the Roman fashion with select weapons, being, as he now was, in possession of a very large quantity of captured arms. He also sent at this time messengers to Carthage by sea with the news of what had happened, this being the first time he had come in touch with the sea since he invaded Italy. The news was received with great rejoicing by the Carthaginians, who hastened to take steps to support in every possible manner the two campaigns in Italy and in Spain.

July 06, Friday
Quintus Fabius Maximus Verrucosus appointed as Dictator in Rome

The Romans had appointed as Dictator Quintus Fabius, a man of admirable judgement and great natural gifts, so much so that still in my own day the members of this family bear the name of Maximus, "Greatest," owing to the achievements and success of this man. A dictator differs from the Consuls in these respects, that while each of the Consuls is attended by twelve lictors, the Dictator has twenty-four, and that while the Consuls require in many matters the co-operation of the Senate, the Dictator is a general with absolute powers, all the magistrates in Rome, except the Tribunes, ceasing to hold office on his appointment. However, I will deal with this subject in greater detail later. At the same time they appointed Marcus Minucius Master of the Horse. The Master of the Horse is subordinate to the Dictator but becomes as it were his successor when the Dictator is otherwise occupied.

July 13, Friday

88 Hannibal now shifting his camp from time to time continued to remain in the country near the Adriatic, and by bathing his horses with old wine, of which there was abundance, he thoroughly set right their mangy condition. In like manner he completely cured his wounded, and made the rest of his men sound in body and ready to perform cheerfully the services that would be required of them. After passing through and

July 17, Tuesday
Defeats the people of Praetutia

devastating the territories of Praetutia,

July 20, Friday
Defeats the people of Hadriana

Hadriana,

July 22, Sunday
Defeats the people of Marrucina

Marrucina, and

July 25, Wednesday
Defeats the people of Frentana

Frentana

July 27, Friday
Marches towards Iapygia

he marched on towards Iapygia. This province is divided among three peoples, the Daunii, Peucetii and Messapii, and

August 02, Thursday
Defeats the people in the territory of the Daunii

it was the territory of the Daunii that Hannibal first invaded.

August 06, Monday

Starting from Luceria, a Roman colony in this district,

August 11, Saturday

he laid waste the surrounding country.

August 20, Monday
Encamps near Vibo

He next encamped near Vibo and

August 28, Tuesday

overran the territory of Argyripa and plundered all Daunia unopposed.

At the same time Fabius on his appointment, after sacrificing to the gods, also took the field with his colleague and the four legions which had been raised for the emergency. Joining near Narnia the army from Ariminum, he relieved Gnaeus the Consul of his command on land and sent him with an escort to Rome with orders to take the steps that circumstances called for should the Carthaginians make any naval movements. Himself with his Master of the Horse taking the whole army under his command, he encamped opposite the Carthaginians near Aecae about six miles from the enemy.

September 08, Saturday
Hears of arrival of Fabius

89 When he learnt that Fabius had arrived, Hannibal, wishing to strike such a blow as would effectually cow the enemy,

September 10, Monday
Places his forces in combat-mode as an enticement for battle with Fabius

led his forces out and drew them up in order of battle at a short distance from the Roman camp, but after waiting some time,

September 12, Wednesday
Retires to his own camp

as nobody came out to meet him, he retired again to his own camp. For Fabius, having determined not to expose himself to any risk or to venture on a battle, but to make the safety of the army under his command his first and chief aim, adhered steadfastly to this purpose. At first, it is true, he was despised for this, and gave people occasion to say that he was playing the coward and was in deadly fear of an engagement, but as time went on, he forced everyone to confess and acknowledge that it was impossible for anyone to deal with the present situation in more sensible and prudent manner. Very soon indeed facts testified to the wisdom of his conduct, and this was no wonder. For the enemy's forces had been trained in actual warfare constantly from their earliest youth, they had a general who had been brought up together with them and was accustomed from childhood to operations in the field, they had won many battles in Spain and had twice in succession beaten the Romans and their allies, and what was most important, they had cast to the winds everything else, and their only hope of safety lay in victory. The circumstances of the Roman army were the exact opposite, and therefore Fabius was not able to meet the enemy in a general battle, as it would evidently result in a reverse, but on due consideration he fell back on those means in which the Romans had the advantage, confined himself to these, and regulated his conduct of the war thereby. These advantages of the Romans lay in inexhaustible supplies of provisions and men.

Early Autumn

90 He, therefore, during the period which followed continued to move parallel to the enemy, always occupying in advance the positions which his knowledge of the country told him were the most advantageous. Having always a plentiful store of provisions in his rear he never allowed his soldiers to forage or to straggle from the camp on any pretext, but keeping them continually massed together watched for such opportunities as time and place afforded. In this manner he continued to take or kill numbers of the enemy, who despising him had strayed far from their own camp in foraging. He acted so in order, on the one hand, to keep on reducing the strictly limited numbers of the enemy, and, on the other, with the view of gradually strengthening and restoring by partial successes the spirits of his own troops, broken as they were by the general reverses. He was, however, not at all disposed to respond to the enemy's challenge and meet him in a set battle. But all this much displeased his colleague Marcus, who, echoing the popular verdict, ran down Fabius to all for his craven and slow conduct of the campaign, while he himself was most eager to risk a battle.

October 02, Tuesday
Crossed the Apennines

The Carthaginians, after ravaging the country I mentioned, crossed the Apennines and

October 04, Thursday
Entered the territory of the Samnites

descended into the territory of the Samnites, which was very fertile and had not for long been visited by war,

October 07, Sunday
Overrun the territory of the Samnites

so that they had such abundance of provisions that they could not succeed either in using or in destroying all their booty.

October 13, Saturday
Overrun the territory of the Beneventum

They also overran the territory of Beneventum, a Roman colony,

October 17, Wednesday
Take the city of Telesia

and took the city of Telesia, which was unwalled and full of all manner of property. The Romans continued to hang on their rear at a distance of one or two days' march, refusing to approach nearer and engage the enemy.

October 22, Monday
Makes a move towards Falernum

Hannibal, consequently, seeing that Fabius, while obviously wishing to avoid battle, had no intention of withdrawing altogether from the open country, made a bold dash at Falernum in the plain of Capua, counting with certainty on one of two alternatives: either he would compel the enemy to fight or make it plain to everybody that he was winning and that the

Romans were abandoning the country to him. Upon this happening he hoped that the towns would be much impressed and hasten to throw off their allegiance to Rome. For up to now, although the Romans had been beaten in two battles, not a single Italian city had revolted to the Carthaginians, but all remained loyal, although some suffered much. From which one may estimate the awe and respect that the allies felt for the Roman state.

91 Hannibal, however, had sufficient reason for reckoning as he did. The plain round Capua is the most celebrated in all Italy, both for its fertility and beauty, and because it is served by those sea-ports at which voyagers to Italy from nearly all parts of the world land. It also contains the most celebrated and finest cities in Italy. On the coast lie Sinuessa, Cyme, and Dicaearchea, and following on these Naples and finally Nuceria. In the interior we find on the north Cales and Teanum and east and south Caudium and Nola, while in the very middle of the plain lies Capua, once the wealthiest of cities. The mythical tale concerning this plain, and other celebrated plains which like it are called Phlegraean, has indeed much semblance of probability; for it was quite natural that they should have been a special cause of strife among the gods owing to their beauty and fertility. Besides the above advantages the whole plain of Capua is strongly protected by nature and difficult of approach, being completely surrounded on one side by the sea and for the greater part by lofty mountain-ranges, through which there are only three passes from the interior, all of them narrow and difficult, one from Samnium, the second from Latium, and the third from the country of the Hirpini.

October 25, Thursday

The Carthaginians, then, by quartering themselves in this plain made of it a kind of theatre, in which they were sure to create a deep impression on all by their unexpected appearance, giving a spectacular exhibition of the timidity of their enemy and themselves demonstrating indisputably that they were in command of the country.

October 26, Friday

92 Such being Hannibal's anticipations, he left Samnium and traversing the pass near the hill called Eribianus encamped beside the river Athyrnus, which approximately cuts this plain in half.

October 27, Saturday

Establishing his camp on the side of the river towards Rome

November 03, Saturday

he overran and plundered the whole plain unmolested.

November 04, Sunday
Fabius shocked by Hannibal's bold move

Fabius, though taken aback by the audacity of this stroke on the part of the enemy, continued all the more to adhere to his deliberate plan. But his colleague Marcus and all the tribunes and centurions in his army, thinking they had caught Hannibal famously, urged him to make all haste to reach the plain and not allow the finest part of the country to be devastated. Fabius did bestir himself to reach the district, sharing in so far the view of the more eager and venturesome spirits,

November 08, Thursday
Fabius observes the Carthaginians

but when he came in view of the enemy on approaching Falernum, while moving along the hills parallel to them so as not to appear to the allies to be abandoning the open country, he did not bring his army down into the plain, avoiding a general action both for the above-mentioned reasons and because the Carthaginians were obviously much his superiors in cavalry.

November 09, Friday

Hannibal, having thus done his best to provoke the Romans by laying the whole plain waste, found himself in possession of a huge amount of booty and decided to withdraw, as he wished not to waste the booty, but to secure it in a place suitable for his winter quarters, so that his army should not only fare sumptuously for the present, but continue to have abundance of provisions.

November 10, Saturday
Fabius sets a plan of ambush

Fabius, divining that his plan was to retire by the same pass by which he had entered, and seeing that owing to its narrowness the place was exceedingly favourable for delivering an attack, stationed about four thousand men at the actual pass, bidding them act at the proper time with all spirit, while availing themselves fully of the advantage of the ground. He himself with the greater part of his army encamped on a hill in front of the pass and overlooking it.

November 11, Sunday
Preparation for Battle

When the Carthaginians arrived and made their camp on the level ground just under the hill, Fabius thought that at least he would be able to carry away their booty without their disputing it and possibly even to put an end to the whole campaign owing to the great advantage his position gave him. He was in fact entirely occupied in considering at what point and how he should avail himself of local conditions, and with what troops he should attack, and from which direction. But while the enemy were making these preparations for the next day, Hannibal, conjecturing that they would act so, gave them no time or leisure to develop their plan, but summoning Hasdrubal, who was in command of the Army Service, ordered him to get as many faggots as possible of any kind of dry wood made promptly and to collect in the front of the camp about two thousand of the strongest plough oxen among all the captured stock. When this had been done, he collected the army servants and pointed out to them a rise in the ground between his own camp and the pass through which he was about to march. For this eminence he ordered them to drive the oxen whenever they received the word as furiously as they could till they reached the top. He next ordered all his men to get their supper and retire to rest early. When the third watch of the night was nearly over he led out the army servants and ordered them bind the fagots to the horns of the oxen. This was soon done as there were plenty of hands, and he now bade them light all the fagots and drive the oxen up to the ridge. Placing his pikemen behind these men, he ordered them to help the drivers up to a certain point, but as soon as the animals were well started on their career, to run along on each side of them and keep them together, making for the higher ground. They were then to occupy the ridge, so that if the enemy advanced to any part of it, they might meet and attack him. At the same time he himself with his heavy-armed troops in front, next them his cavalry, next the captured cattle, and finally the Spaniards and Celts, made for the narrow gorge of the pass. The Romans who were guarding the gorge, thinking that Hannibal was pressing on rapidly in that direction, left the narrow part of the pass and advanced to the hill to meet the enemy. But when they got near the oxen they were entirely puzzled by the lights, fancying that they were about to encounter something much more formidable than the reality. When the pikemen came up, both forces skirmished with each other for a short time, and then when the oxen rushed in among them they drew apart and remained on the heights waiting until day should break, not being able to understand what was the matter. Fabius, partly because he was at a loss to know what was occurring, and as Homer says, deeming it to be a trick, and partly because he adhered to his former resolve not to risk or hazard a general engagement, remained quite in his camp waiting for daylight. Meanwhile Hannibal, whose plan had been entirely successful, brought his army and all his booty safely through the gorge, those who had been guarding the difficult passage having quitted their post.

November 12, Monday
Battle of Ager Falernus (Battle of the Falernian Territory)

When at daybreak he saw the Romans on the hill drawn up opposite his pikemen, he sent there some Spaniards as a reinforcement. Attacking the Romans they killed about a thousand and easily relieved and brought down their own light infantry.

November 13, Tuesday

Hannibal, having thus effected his retirement from Falernum, remained now safely in camp and began to take thought where and how he should establish his winter quarters. He had spread great terror and perplexity through all the cities and peoples of Italy.

November 17, Saturday
Fabius leaves for Rome

Fabius, though generally reproached for his craven conduct in letting the enemy escape from such a situation, still did not abandon his policy. But a few days afterwards he was compelled to leave for Rome to perform certain sacrifices and handed over his legions to his Master of the Horse, enjoining on him strictly, in taking leave, not to attach so much importance to damaging the enemy as to avoiding disaster for himself. Marcus, instead of paying any attention to this advice, was, even while Fabius was tendering it, entirely wrapped up in the project of risking a great battle.

95 Such was the position of affairs in Italy. Contemporaneously with these events Hasdrubal, the Carthaginian commander in Spain, after fitting out during the winter the thirty ships his brother had left him, and manning ten others, put out at the beginning of summer from New Carthage with his fleet of forty decked ships, appointing Hamilcar his admiral. At the same time he collected his troops from their winter quarters and took the field. His fleet sailed close to the shore and his army marched along the beach, his object being to halt with both forces near the Ebro. Gnaeus, conjecturing that this was the plan of the Carthaginians, first of all designed to quit his winter quarters and meet them both by land and sea, but on learning the strength of their forces and the extensive scale of their preparations he renounced the project of meeting them by land, and manning thirty-five ships and embarking on them as marines the men from his army most suited for this service, appeared off the Ebro two days after sailing from Tarraco. Anchoring at a distance of about eighty stades from the enemy he sent on two swift Massaliot ships to reconnoitre, for these used to head the line both in sailing and in battle, and there was absolutely no service they were not ready to render. Indeed if any people have given generous support to the Romans it is the people of Marseilles both on many subsequent occasions and especially in the Hannibalic War. When the scouts reported that the enemy's fleet was anchored off the mouth of the river, he weighed anchor and advanced rapidly, wishing to fall upon them suddenly. Hasdrubal, to whom his lookout men had given early notice of the approach of the enemy, drew up his land forces on the beach and ordered his crews to embark. The Romans being now close at hand, he gave the signal for battle, having decided on a naval action. The Carthaginians on meeting the enemy contested the victory only for a short time and then began to give way. For the covering military force on the beach did not benefit them so much by the confidence it inspired as it damaged them by ensuring an easy and safe retreat. After losing two ships with all their crews and the oars and marines of four others, they fell back on the shore. On the Romans pursuing them vigorously they ran their ships aground and leaping out of them took refuge with the troops. The Romans very boldly approached the shore, and taking in tow such ships as were in a condition to float, sailed off in high spirits, having beaten the enemy at the first onslaught, established their supremacy at sea and possessed themselves of five and twenty of the enemy's ships.

Owing to this success the prospects of the Romans in Spain began thenceforth to look brighter. But the Carthaginians, on the news of their defeat, at once manned and dispatched seventy ships, regarding the command of the sea as necessary for all their projects. These ships touched first at Sardinia and then at Pisa in Italy, the commander believing they would meet Hannibal there, but on learning that the Romans had at once put to sea from Rome itself with a hundred and twenty quinqueremes to attack them, they sailed back again to Sardinia and thence to Carthage. Gnaeus Servilius, the commander of this Roman fleet, followed up the Carthaginians for a certain distance, believing he would overtake them, but on being left a long way behind, he gave up the chase. He first of all put in at Lilybaeum in Sicily and afterwards sailed to the African island of Cercina, which he quitted after receiving from the inhabitants a sum of money on condition of his not laying the country waste. On his return voyage he possessed himself of the island of Cossyrus, and leaving a garrison in the small town returned to Lilybaeum. After laying up his fleet in harbour there, he very shortly went off to join the land forces.

97 The Senate on hearing of Gnaeus Scipio's success in the naval battle, thinking it advantageous or rather imperative not to neglect the affairs of Spain but to keep up the pressure on the Carthaginians and increase their forces, got ready twenty ships, and placing them, as they had originally decided, under the command of Publius Scipio, dispatched him at once to join his brother Gnaeus and operate in Spain together with him. For they were very apprehensive lest the Carthaginians should master that country, and, collecting abundance of supplies and soldiers, make a more serious effort to regain the command of the sea and thus support the invasion of Italy by sending troops and money to Hannibal. Treating this war, then, also as of great moment they dispatched Publius with his fleet, and on reaching Iberia and joining his brother he rendered great service in their joint operations. For the Romans, who had never before dared to cross the Ebro, but had been content with the friendship and alliance of the peoples on its north bank, now crossed it, and for the first time ventured to aim at acquiring dominion on the other side, chance also greatly contributing to advance their prospects in the following manner.

When after overawing the Iberian tribes dwelling near the crossing of the Ebro they reached Saguntum, they encamped at a distance of about five miles from the town near the temple of Venus, choosing a place well situated both as regards security from the enemy and facility for obtaining supplies from the sea, since their fleet was coasting down together with them.

98 Here a remarkable development of events occurred. When Hannibal was starting on his march for Italy he took as hostages from those cities in Iberia on which he did not rely the sons of their principal men, and all these he placed in Saguntum owing to the strength of the place and the loyalty of the officers he left in charge of it. Now there was a certain Iberian named Abilyx, second to none in Iberia in rank and wealth and with the reputation of being more devoted and loyal to the Carthaginians than anyone else. Reviewing the situation and thinking that the prospects of the Romans were now the brightest, he reasoned with himself in a manner thoroughly Spanish and barbarian on the question of betraying the hostages. For, being convinced that if he both rendered the Romans a timely service and gave them proof of his good faith, he would become very influential with them, he formed the scheme of playing the traitor to the Carthaginians and handing over the hostages to the Romans. The Carthaginian general, Bostar, whom Hasdrubal had sent to oppose the Romans if they tried to cross the Ebro, but who had not ventured to do so, had now retreated and encamped between Saguntum and the sea. Abilyx, perceiving that he was of a guileless and mild disposition and placed full confidence in himself, approached him on the subject of the hostages, saying that now the Romans had once crossed the river it was no longer possible for the Carthaginians to control the Iberians by fear, but that present circumstances required the goodwill of all the subject peoples. So now, when the Romans had approached and were encamped close to Saguntum and the city was in danger, if he brought the hostages out and restored them to their parents and cities, he would in the first place frustrate the ambitious project of the Romans, who were bent on taking just the same step if they got the hostages into their hands, and further he would elicit the gratitude of all the Iberians to the Carthaginians by thus foreseeing the future and taking thought for the safety of the hostages. This act of grace, he said, would be very much enhanced, if Bostar would let him take the matter in hand personally. For in restoring the children to the cities not only would he gain him the goodwill of their parents but that of the mass of the people, by thus bringing actually before their eyes this evidence of the magnanimous conduct of Carthage toward her allies. He told Bostar also that he could count on many presents to himself from those to whom their children were returned; for each and all, on thus unexpectedly receiving back their dearest, would view with each other in heaping benefits on the author of the measure. By these and more words to the like effect he persuaded Bostar to assent to his proposal.

99 For the present he left to return home, fixing the day on which he would come with his followers to escort the children. At night he went to the Roman camp, and having found some of the Iberians who were serving in the army, gained access through them to the generals. Pointing out at some length how the Iberians if they recovered their hostages would with one impulse go over to the Romans, he undertook to give up the children to them. Publius, to whom the project was exceedingly welcome, having promised him a great reward, he now left for his own country, having fixed a day and agreed on the hour and place at which those who were to take over the hostages should await him. After this, taking his most intimate friends with him, he came to Bostar; and on the children being handed over to him from Saguntum, he sallied out from the town by night as if to keep the matter secret, and marching along the enemies' entrenched camp reached the appointed place at the appointed hour and delivered all the hostages to the Roman generals. Publius conferred great honours on Abilyx, and employed him in the restoration of the hostages to their respective countries, sending certain of his friends with him. Going from city to city, and bringing, by the repatriation of the children, the gentleness and magnanimity of the Romans into manifest contrast with the suspiciousness and harshness of the Carthaginians, at the same time exhibiting the example of his own change of sides, he induced many of the Iberians to become allies of Rome. Bostar was judged in thus handing over the hostages to the enemy to have acted more like a child than became his years, and was in serious danger of his life. For the present both sides, as the season was now advanced, broke up their forces for the winter; chance in this matter of the children having materially contributed to assist the projects the Romans had in view.

100 Such was the position of affairs in Spain.

November 19, Monday
Search for winter quarters

Hannibal, whom we left in Italy looking out for winter quarters, learning from his scouts that there was plenty of corn in the country round Luceria and Geronium, and that the best place for collecting supplies was Geronium, decided to winter there and advanced to this district,

November 20, Tuesday
Passes Mount Libyrnus

marching past Mount Libyrnus.

November 21, Wednesday
Arrives at Geronium (corresponding to modern-day Molise and 37km or 200 stades from Luceria) and sends messages for their stipulation

On reaching Geronium, which is two hundred stades from Luceria, he at first sent messages to the inhabitants asking for their alliance and offering pledges of the advantages he promised them, but as they paid not attention to them

November 23, Friday
Lays siege to Geronium

he began the siege.

November 27, Tuesday
Invades Geronium

he began the siege.

He soon took the city, upon which he put the inhabitants to the sword, but kept the walls and most of the houses uninjured, intending to use them as corn magazine for the winter. He encamped his army before the town, fortifying his camp with a trench and palisade.

December 01, Saturday
Begins local foraging raids

When he had completed this he sent two divisions of his army out to gather corn, ordering each to bring in each day for its own use the quantity imposed by those in charge of the commissariat. With the remaining third he guarded the camp and covered the foraging parties here and there. As most of the country was flat and easy to overrun, and the foragers were one might say infinite in number, and the weather was very favourable for fetching in the grain, an enormous quantity was collected every day.

101 Minucius on taking over the command from Fabius at first followed the Carthaginians along the hills, always expecting to encounter them when attempting to cross. But on hearing that Hannibal had already occupied Geronium, and was foraging in the district, and had established himself in a fortified camp before the city,

December 06, Thursday
Minucius descends from the hills near Geronium

he turned and descended from the hills by a ridge that slopes down to the town. Arriving at the height in the territory of Larinum called Calena he encamped there, being eager at all hazards to engage the enemy. Hannibal, seeing the approach of the Romans, left the third part of his army to forage, and taking the other two-thirds advanced sixteen stades from the town and encamped on a hill with the view of overawing the enemy and affording protection to the foragers. There was a certain hillock between the two armies, and observing that it lay close to the enemy's camp and commanded it, he sent two thousand of his pikemen in the night to occupy it.

December 07, Friday
Small skirmish with Roman victory

Marcus, catching sight of them at daybreak, led out his light-armed troops and attacked the hill. A brisk skirmish took place in which the Romans were victorious, and afterwards they transferred their whole army to this hill.

December 08, Saturday
Army kept in the camp

Hannibal for a certain time kept the whole of his forces within the camp owing to the propinquity of the enemy;

December 12, Wednesday
Battle at Geronium

but after some days he was compelled to tell off a portion to pasture the animals, and send others to forage for corn, as he was anxious, according to his original plan, to avoid loss in the live stock he had captured and to collect as much corn as possible, so that for the whole winter there should be plenty of everything both for his men and also for the horses and pack-animals; for it was on his cavalry above all that he placed reliance.

102 Minucius, remarking that the greater number of the enemy were dispersed over the country on these services, chose the time when the day was at its height to lead out his forces, and on approaching the enemy's camp, drew up his legionaries, and dividing his cavalry and light-armed infantry into several troops sent them out to attack the foragers, with orders to take no prisoners. Hannibal hereupon found himself in a very difficult position, being neither strong enough to march out and meet the enemy nor able to go to the assistance of those of his men who were scattered over the country. The Romans who had been dispatched to attack the foraging parties, killed numbers of them, and finally the troops drawn up in line reached such a pitch of contempt for the enemy that they began to pull down the palisade and very nearly stormed the Carthaginian camp. Hannibal was in sore straits, but notwithstanding the tempest that had thus overtaken him he continued to drive off all assailants and with difficulty to hold his camp, until Hasdrubal, with those who had fled from the country for refuge to the camp before Geronium, about four thousand in number, came to succour him. He now regained a little confidence, and sallying from the camp drew up his troops a short distance in front of it and with difficulty averted the impending peril. Minucius, after killing many of the enemy in the engagement at the camp and still more throughout the country, now retired, but with great hopes for the future, and

December 13, Thursday
Day after the Battle at Geronium

next day, on the Carthaginians evacuating their camp, occupied it himself. For Hannibal, fearful lest the Romans, finding the camp at Geronium deserted at night, should capture his baggage and stores, decided to return and encamp there again. Henceforth the Carthaginians were much more cautious and guarded in foraging, while the Romans on the contrary, foraged with greater confidence and temerity.

December 15, Saturday
News of the Battle at Geronium reaches Rome

103 People in Rome, when an exaggerated account of this success reached the city, were overjoyed, partly because this change for the better relieved their general despondency, and in the next place because they inferred that the former inaction and disheartenment of their army was not the result of any want of courage in the soldiers, but of the excessive caution of the general. All therefore found fault with Fabius, accusing him of not making a bold use of his opportunities, while

December 19, Wednesday
Marcus Minucius Rufus appointed joint dictator with Fabius

Marcus's reputation rose so much owing to this event that they took an entirely unprecedented step, investing him like the Dictator with absolute power, in the belief that he would very soon put an end to the war. So two Dictators were actually appointed for the same field of action, a thing which had never before happened at Rome.

December 21, Friday
Minucius hears of his promotion

When Minucius was informed of his popularity at home and the office given him by the people's decree, he grew twice as eager to run risks and take some bold action against the enemy.

December 23, Sunday
Fabius returns to the army

Fabius now returned to the army wholly unchanged by recent circumstances, and adhering even more firmly than before to his original determination. Observing that Minucius was unduly elated and was jealously opposing him in every way and altogether strongly disposed to risk a battle, he offered for his choice, either that he should be in full command on alternate days, or that he should take half the army and use his own legions in any way he thought fit. Minucius having readily agreed to the division of the army, they divided it and encamped apart at a distance of about twelve stades from each other.

December 27, Thursday
Hannibal devises a plan

104 Hannibal, partly from what he heard from prisoners and partly from what he saw was going on, was aware of the rivalry of the two generals and of Marcus' impulsiveness and ambition. Considering, then, that the present circumstances of the enemy were not against him but in his favour, he turned his attention to Minucius, being anxious to put a stop to his venturesomeness and anticipate his offensive. There was a small eminence between his own camp and that of Minucius capable of being used against either of them, and this he decided to occupy. While knowing that owing to his previous achievement Minucius would instantly advance to frustrate this project, he devised the following stratagem.

December 29, Saturday
Ambush plan is enacted at night

The ground round the hill was treeless but had many irregularities and hollows of every description in it, and he sent out at night to the most suitable positions for ambuscade, in bodies of two or three hundred, five hundred horse and about five thousand light-armed and other infantry. In order that they should not be observed in the early morning by the Romans who were going out to forage, he occupied the hill with his light-armed troops as soon as it was daybreak. Minucius, seeing this and thinking a favourable chance, sent out at once his light infantry with orders to engage the enemy and dispute the position. Afterwards he sent his cavalry too and next followed in person leading his legions in close order, as on the former occasion, operating exactly in the same manner as then.

December 30, Sunday
Defeat of the Romans under the command of Minucius

105 The day was just dawning, and the minds and eyes of all were engrossed in the battle on the hill, so that no one suspected that the ambuscade had been posted. Hannibal kept constantly sending reinforcements to his men on the hill, and when he very shortly followed himself with his cavalry and the rest of his force, the cavalry on both sides soon came into action. Upon this, the Roman light infantry were forced off the field by the numbers of the Carthaginian horse, and, falling back on the legions, threw them into confusion, while at the same time, on the signal being given to those lying in ambush, they appeared from all directions and attacked, upon which not only the Roman light infantry but their whole army found itself in a most perilous position. It was now that Fabius, seeing the state of matters and seriously fearing a total disaster, came up in haste with his own army to assist. On his approach the Romans again plucked up courage, although they had now entirely broken their ranks, and collecting round the standards retreated and took refuge under cover of Fabius' force after losing many of their light-armed troops, but still more of the legionaries and the very best men among them. Hannibal, being afraid of the legions, which, quite fresh and in admirable order, had come to the help of their comrades, abandoned the pursuit and brought the battle to a close. To those who were actually present at the action it was evident that all was lost

HUTAN ASHRAFIAN

by the rashness of Minucius, and that now, as on previous occasions, all had been saved by the caution of Fabius.

92

216 BC

January 02, Wednesday
News of the defeat arrives in Rome and the Fabian strategy appreciated

And to those in Rome it became indisputably clear how widely the foresight, good sense, and calm calculation of a general differ from the recklessness and bravado of a mere soldier. The Romans, however, had received a practical lesson, and again fortifying a single camp, joined their forces in it, and in future paid due attention to Fabius and his orders.

January 04, Friday
Trench is dug between the Carthaginians and Roman armies

The Carthaginians dug a trench between the hill and their own camp, and erecting a stockade round the hill, which was now in their hands, and placing a garrison on it, made their preparations henceforth for the winter undisturbed.

January 12, Saturday
Consular elections in Rome

106 The time for the consular elections was now approaching, and the Romans elected Lucius Aemilius Paulus and Gaius Terentius Varro. On their appointment, the Dictators laid down their office, and the Consuls of the previous year, Gnaeus Servilius and Marcus Regulus — who had been appointed after the death of Flaminius — were invested with proconsular authority by Aemilius, and taking command in the field directed the operations of their forces as they thought fit.

January 18, Friday
Aemilius consults with the senate

Aemilius after consulting with the Senate

January 22, Tuesday
Aemilius enrols soldiers for the army

at once enrolled the soldiers still wanting to make up the total levy and

January 28, Monday
Roman soldiers dispatched to the army awaiting battle with the Carthaginians

dispatched them to the front, expressly ordering Servilius on no account to risk a general engagement, but to skirmish vigorously and unintermittently so as to train the lads and give them confidence for a general battle; for they thought the chief cause of their late reverses lay in their having employed newly raised and quite untrained levies. The Consuls also gave a legion to the Praetor Lucius Postumius, and sent him to Cisalpine Gaul to create a diversion among those Celts who were serving with Hannibal, they took measures for the return of the fleet that was wintering at Lilybaeum and sent the generals in Spain all the supplies of which they had need. The Consuls and Senate were thus occupied with these and other preparations, and Servilius, on receiving orders from the Consuls, conducted all petty operations as they directed. I shall therefore not make further mention of these, for nothing decisive or noteworthy was done owing to these orders and owing to circumstances, but only numerous skirmishes and minor engagements took place in which the Roman commanders had the advantage, their conduct of the campaign being generally thought to have been both courageous and skilful.

107 All through the winter and spring the two armies remained encamped opposite each other,

July 01, Monday
Leaves camp near Geronium (near modern-day Molise). This took place during the summer manual crop harvest in central and southern Italy (see Cecchini M, Colantoni A, Massantini R, Monarca D. Estimation of the risks of thermal stress due to the microclimate for manual fruit and vegetable harvesters in central Italy. J Agric Saf Health. 2010 Jul;16(3):141-59). Summer in 216 BC had begun at the first visibility of the Pleiades on May 25).

and it was not until the season was advanced enough for them to get supplies from the year's crops that Hannibal moved his forces out of the camp near Geronium.

July 07, Monday
Seized citadel at Cannae (the distance between Cannae and Molise is approximately 240km)

Judging that it was in his interest to compel the enemy to fight by every means in his power, he seized on the citadel of a town called Cannae, in which the Romans had collected the corn and other supplies from the country round Canusium, conveying hence to their camp from time to time enough to supply their wants.

July 08, Monday
Roman army send multiple messages of the fall of the Cannae citadel to Rome

The city itself had previously been razed, but the capture now of the citadel and stores caused no little commotion in the Roman army; for they were distressed at the fall of the place not only owing to the loss of their supplies, but because it commanded the surrounding district. They continued, therefore, to send constant messages to Rome asking how they should act, stating that if they approached the enemy they would not be able to escape a battle, as the country was being pillaged and the temper of all the allies was uncertain.

July 14, Sunday
Response of the Roman Senate

The Senate decided to give the enemy battle, but they ordered Servilius to wait, and dispatched the Consuls to the front. It was to Aemilius that the eyes of all were directed; and they placed their chiefest hope in him, owing to his general high character, and because a few years previously he was thought to have conducted the Illyrian war with courage and advantage to the state. They decided to bring eight legions into the field, a thing which had never been done before by the Romans, each legion consisting of about five thousand men apart from the allies. For, as I previously explained, they invariably employ four legions, each numbering about four thousand foot and two hundred horse, but on occasions of exceptional gravity they raise the number of foot in each legion to five thousand and that of the cavalry to three hundred. They make the number of the allied infantry equal to that of the Roman legions, but, as a rule, the allied cavalry are three times as numerous as the Roman. They give each of the Consuls half of the allies and two legions when they dispatch them to the field, and most of their wars are decided by one Consul with two legions and the above number of allies, it being only on rare occasions that they employ all their forces at one time and in one battle. But now they were so alarmed and anxious as to the future that they decided to bring into action not four legions but eight.

July 16, Tuesday
Aemilius dispatched (Canne is approximately 400km from Rome)

108 Therefore after exhorting Aemilius and putting before his eyes the magnitude of the results which in either event the battle would bring about, they dispatched him with orders to decide the issue, when the time came, bravely and worthily of his country.

July 26, Friday
Aemilius gives a speech to the Roman army

On reaching the army he assembled the soldiers and conveyed to them the decision of the Senate, addressing them in a manner befitting the occasion and in words that evidently sprang from his heart. The greater part of his speech was devoted to accounting for the former reverses, for it was particularly the impression created by these that made the men disheartened and in need of encouragement. He attempted therefore to impress upon them, that while not one or two but many causes could be found owing to which the previous battles resulted in defeat, there was at present, if they behaved like men, no reason at all left why they should not be victorious "For then," he said, "the two Consuls never gave battle with their united armies, nor were the forces they disposed of well trained, but raw levies who had never looked danger in the face. But the most important consideration of all is that our troops were then so ignorant of the enemy that one might almost say they ventured on decisive battles with them without ever having set eyes on them. Those who were worsted at the Trebia had only arrived from Sicily the day before, and

July 27, Saturday

at daybreak on the following morning went into action, while those who fought in Etruria not only had not seen their enemies before, but could not even see them in the battle itself owing to the condition of the atmosphere. But now all the circumstances are precisely the opposite of what they were then.

109 For in the first place we, the Consuls, are both present, and are not only about to share your perils ourselves but have given you also the Consuls of last year to stand by you and participate in the struggle. And you yourselves have not only seen how the enemy are armed, how they dispose their forces, and what is their strength, but for two years now you have been fighting with them nearly every day. As, therefore, all the conditions are now the reverse of those in the battles I spoke of, we may anticipate that the result of the present battle will likewise be the opposite. For it would be a strange or rather indeed impossible thing, that after meeting your enemies on equal terms in so many separate skirmishes and in most cases being victorious, now when you confront them by more than two to one you should be beaten. Therefore, my men, every measure having been taken to secure victory for you, one thing alone is wanting, your own zeal and resolution, and as to this it is not, I think, fitting that I should exhort you further. For those who in some countries serve for hire or for those who are about to fight for their neighbours by the terms of an alliance, the moment of greatest peril is during the battle itself, but the result makes little difference to them, and in such a case exhortation is necessary. But those who like you are about to fight not for others, but for yourselves, your country, and your wives and children, and for whom the results that will ensue are of vastly more importance than the present peril, require not to be exhorted to do their duty but only to be reminded of it. For what man is there who would not wish before all things to conquer in the struggle, or if this be not possible, to die fighting rather than witness the outrage and destruction of all that is dearest to him? Therefore, my men, even without these words of mine, fix your eyes on the difference between defeat and victory and on all that must follow upon either, and enter on this battle as if not your country's legions but her existence were at stake. For if the issue of the day be adverse, she has no further resources to overcome her foes; but she has centred all her power and spirit in you, and in you lies her sole hope of safety. Do not cheat her, then, of this hope, but now pay the debt of gratitude you owe to her, and make it clear to all men that our former defeats were not due to the Romans being less brave than the Carthaginians, but to the inexperience of those who fought for us then and to the force of circumstances." Having addressed the troops in these words Aemilius dismissed them.

July 28, Sunday

110 Next day the Consuls broke up their camp and advanced towards the place where they heard that of the enemy was.

July 29, Monday

Coming in view of them on the second day, they encamped at a distance of about fifty stadia from them. Aemilius, seeing that the district round was flat and treeless, was opposed to attacking the enemy there as they were superior in cavalry, his advice being to lure them on by advancing into a country where the battle would be decided rather by the infantry. As Terentius, owing to his inexperience, was of the contrary opinion, difficulties and disputes arose between the generals, one of the most pernicious things possible.

July 30, Tuesday

Terentius was in command next day — the two Consuls according to the usual practice commanding on alternate days — and he broke up his camp and advanced with the object of approaching the enemy in spite of Aemilius's strong protests and efforts to prevent him. Hannibal met him with his light-armed troops and cavalry and surprising him while still on the march disordered the Romans much. They met, however, the first charge by advancing some of their heavy infantry, and afterwards sending forwards also their javelineers and cavalry got the better in the whole engagement, as the Carthaginians had no considerable covering force, while they themselves had some companies of their legions fighting mixed with the light-armed troops. The fall of night now made them draw off from each other, the attack of the Carthaginians not having had the success they hoped.

July 31, Wednesday

Next day, Aemilius, who neither judged it advisable to fight nor could now withdraw the army in safety, encamped with two-thirds of it on the bank of the river Aufidus. This is the only river which traverses the Apennines, the long chain of mountains separating all the Italian streams, those on one side descending to the Tyrrhenian sea and those on the other to the Adriatic. The Aufidus, however, runs right through these mountains, having its source on the side of Italy turned to the Tyrrhenian Sea and falling into the Adriatic. For the remaining portion of his army he fortified a position on the farther side of the river, to the east of the ford, at a distance of about ten stadia from his own camp and rather more from that of the enemy, intending thus to cover the foraging parties from his main camp across the river and harass those of the Carthaginians.

111 Hannibal now seeing that it was imperative for him to give battle and attack the enemy, and careful lest his soldiers might be disheartened by this recent reverse, thought that the occasion demanded some words of exhortation and called a meeting of the men. When they were assembled he bade them all look at the country round, and asked them what greater boon they could in their present circumstances crave from the gods, if they had their choice, than to fight the decisive battle on such ground, greatly superior as they were to the enemy in cavalry. As they could see this for themselves they all applauded and, he continued: "In the first place then thank the gods for this; for it is they who working to aid you to victory have led the enemy on to such ground, and next thank myself for compelling them to fight, a thing they can no longer avoid, and to fight here where the advantages are manifestly ours. I do not think it at all my duty to exhort you at further length to be of good heart and eager for the battle, and this is why. Then, when you had no experience of what a battle with the Romans was, this was necessary, and I often addressed you, giving examples, but now that you have beyond dispute beaten the Romans consecutively in three great battles, what words of mine could confirm your courage more than your own deeds? For by these former battles you have gained possession of the country and all its wealth, even as I promised you, and not a word I spoke but has proved true; and the coming battle will be for the cities and their wealth. Your victory will make you at once masters of all Italy, and through this one battle you will be freed from your present toil, you will possess yourselves of all the vast wealth of Rome, and will be lords and masters of all men and all things. Therefore no more words are wanted, but deeds; for if it be the will of the gods I am confident that I shall fulfill my promises forthwith." After he had spoken further to this effect, the army applauded him heartily, whereupon he thanked them and acknowledging their spirit dismissed them, and immediately pitched his camp, placing his entrenchments by the same bank of the river with the larger camp of the enemy.

August 01, Thursday

112 Next day he ordered all his troops to look to their persons and their accoutrements, and on the day following he drew up his army along the river with the evident intention of giving battle as soon as possible. Aemilius was not pleased with the ground, and seeing that the Carthaginians would soon have to shift their camp in order to obtain supplies, kept quiet, after securing his two camps by covering forces. Hannibal, after waiting for some time without anyone coming out to meet him, withdrew again the rest of his army into their intrenchments, but sent out the Numidians to intercept the water-bearers from the lesser Roman camp. When the Numidians came up to the actual palisade of the camp and prevented the men from watering, not only was this a further stimulus to Terentius, but the soldiers displayed great eagerness for battle and ill brooked further delay. For nothing is more trying to men in general than prolonged suspense, but when the issue has once been decided we make a shift to endure patiently all that men regard as the depth of misery.

When the news reached Rome that the armies were encamped opposite each other and that engagements between the outposts occurred every day, there was the utmost excitement and fear in the city, as most people dreaded the result owing to their frequent previous reverses, and foresaw and anticipated in imagination the consequences of total defeat. All the oracles that had ever been delivered to them were in men's mouths, every temple and every house was full of signs and prodigies, so that vows, sacrifices, supplicatory processions and litanies pervaded the town. For in seasons of danger the Romans are much given to propitiating both gods and men, and there is nothing at such times in rites of the kind that they regard as unbecoming or beneath their dignity.

August 02, Friday
Battle of Cannae

113 Next day it was Terentius' turn to take the command, and just after sunrise he began to move his forces out of both camps. Crossing the river with those from the larger camp he at once put them in order of battle, drawing up those from the other camp next to them in the same line, the whole army facing south. He stationed the Roman cavalry close to the river on the right wing and the foot next to them in the same line, placing the maniples closer together than was formerly the usage and making the depth of each many times exceed its front. The allied horse he drew up on his left wing, and in front of the whole force at some distance he placed his light-armed troops. The whole army, including the allies, numbered about eighty thousand foot and rather more than six thousand horse. Hannibal at the same time sent his slingers and pikemen over the river and stationed them in front, and leading the rest of his forces out of camp he crossed the stream in two places and drew them up opposite the enemy. On his left close to the river he placed his Spanish and Celtic horse facing the Roman cavalry, next these half his heavy-armed Africans, then the Spanish and Celtic infantry, and after them the other half of the Africans, and finally, on his right wing, his Numidian horse. After thus drawing up his whole army in a straight line, he took the central companies of the Spaniards and Celts and advanced with them, keeping rest of them in contact with these companies, but gradually falling off, so as to produce a crescent-shaped formation, the line of the flanking companies growing thinner as it was prolonged, his object being to employ the Africans as a reserve force and to begin the action with the Spaniards and Celts.

114 The Africans were armed in the Roman fashion, Hannibal having equipped them with the choicest of the arms captured in the previous battles. The shields of the Spaniards and Celts were very similar, but they swords were entirely different, those of the Spaniards thrusting with as deadly effect as they cut, but the Gaulish sword being only able to slash and requiring a long sweep to do so. As they were drawn up in alternate companies, the Gauls naked and the Spaniards in short tunics bordered with purple, their national dress, they presented a strange and impressive appearance. The Carthaginian cavalry numbered about ten thousand, and their infantry, including the Celts, did not much exceed forty thousand. The Roman right wing was under the command of Aemilius, the left under that of Terentius, and the centre under the Consuls of the previous year, Marcus Atilius and Gnaeus Servilius. Hasdrubal commanded the Carthaginian left, Hanno the right, and Hannibal himself with his brother Mago the centre. Since the Roman army, as I said, faced south and the Carthaginians north, they were neither of them inconvenienced by the rising sun.

115 the advanced guards were the first to come into action, and at first when only the light infantry were engaged neither side had the advantage; but when the Spanish and Celtic horse on the left wing came into collision with the Roman cavalry, the struggle that ensued was truly barbaric; for there were none of the normal wheeling evolutions, but having once met they dismounted and fought man to man. The Carthaginians finally got the upper hand, killed most of the enemy in the mellay, all the Romans fighting with desperate bravery, and began to drive the rest along the river, cutting them down mercilessly, and it was now that the heavy infantry on each side took the place of the light-armed troops and met. For a time the Spaniards and Celts kept their ranks and struggled bravely with the Romans, but soon, borne down by the weight of the legions, they gave way and fell back, breaking up the crescent. The Roman maniples, pursuing them furiously, easily penetrated the enemy's front, since the Celts were deployed in a thin line while they themselves had crowded up from the wings to the centre where the fighting was going on. For the centres and wings did not come into action simultaneously, but the centres first, as the Celts were drawn up in a crescent and a long way in advance of their wings, the convex face of the crescent being turned towards the enemy. The Romans, however, following up the Celts and pressing on to the centre and that part of the enemy's line which was giving way, progressed so far that they now had the heavy-armed Africans on both of their flanks. Hereupon the Africans on the right wing facing to the left and then beginning from the right charged upon the enemy's flank, while those on the left faced to the right and dressing by the left, did the same, the situation itself indicating to them how to act. The consequence was that, as Hannibal had designed, the Romans, straying too far in pursuit of the Celts, were caught between the two divisions of the enemy, and they now no longer kept their compact formation but turned singly or in companies to deal with the enemy who was falling on their flanks.

116 Aemilius, though he had been on the right wing from the outset and had taken part in the cavalry action, was still safe and sound; but wishing to act up to what he had said in his address to the troops, and to be present himself at the fighting, and seeing that the decision of the battle lay mainly with the legions, he rode along to the centre of the whole line, where he not only threw himself personally into the combat and exchanged blows with the enemy but kept cheering on and exhorting his men. Hannibal, who had been in this part of the field since the commencement of the battle, did likewise.

The Numidians meanwhile on the right wing, attacking the cavalry opposite them on the Roman left, neither gained any great advantage nor suffered any serious loss owing to their peculiar mode of fighting, but they kept the enemy's cavalry out of action by drawing them off and attacking them from all sides at once. Hasdrubal, having by this time cut up very nearly all the enemy's cavalry by the river, came up from the left to help the Numidians, and now the Roman allied horse, seeing that they were going to be charged by him, broke and fled. Hasdrubal at this juncture appears to have acted with great skill and prudence; for in view of the fact that the Numidians were very numerous and most efficient and formidable when in pursuit of a flying foe he left them to deal with the Roman cavalry and led his squadrons on to where the infantry were engaged with the object of supporting the Africans. Attacking the Roman legions in the rear and delivering repeated charges at various points all at once, he raised the spirits of the Africans and cowed and dismayed the Romans. It was here that Lucius Aemilius fell in the thick of the fight after receiving several dreadful wounds, and of him we may say that if there ever was a man who did his duty by his country both all through his life and in these last times, it was he. The Romans as long as they could turn and present a front on every side to the enemy, held out, but as the outer ranks continued to fall, and the rest were gradually huddled in and surrounded, they finally all were killed where they stood, among them Marcus and Gnaeus, the Consuls of the preceding year, who had borne themselves in the battle like brave men worthy of Rome. While this murderous combat was going on, the Numidians following up the flying cavalry killed most of them and unseated others. A few escaped to Venusia, among them being the Consul Gaius Terentius, who disgraced himself by his flight and in his tenure of office had been most unprofitable to his country.

117 Such was the outcome of the battle at Cannae between the Romans and Carthaginians, a battle in which both the victors and the vanquished displayed conspicuous bravery, as was evinced by the facts. For of the six thousand cavalry, seventy escaped to Venusia with Terentius, and about three hundred of the allied horse reached different cities in scattered groups. Of the infantry about ten thousand were captured fighting but not in the actual battle, while only perhaps three thousand escaped from the field to neighbouring towns. All the rest, numbering about seventy thousand, died bravely. Both on this occasion and on former ones their numerous cavalry had contributed most to the victory of the Carthaginians, and it demonstrated to posterity that in times of war it is better to give battle with half as many infantry as the enemy and an overwhelming force of cavalry than to be in all respects his equal. Of Hannibal's army there fell about four thousand Celts, fifteen hundred Spaniards and Africans and two hundred cavalry.

The Romans who were made prisoners were not in the battle for the following reason. Lucius had left a force of ten thousand foot in his own camp, in order that, if Hannibal, neglecting his camp, employed his whole army in the field, they might during the battle gain entrance there and capture all the enemy's baggage: if, on the other hand, Hannibal, guessing this danger, left a strong garrison in the camp, the force opposed to the Romans would be reduced in numbers. The circumstances of their capture were more or less as follows. Hannibal had left an adequate force to guard his camp, and when the battle opened, the Romans, as they had been ordered, delivered an assault on this force. At first they held out, but as they were beginning to be hard pressed, Hannibal, who was now victorious in every part of the field, came to their assistance, and routing the Romans shut them up in their camp. He killed two thousand of them and afterwards made all the rest prisoners. The Numidians also reduced the various strongholds throughout the country which had given shelter to the flying enemy and brought in the fugitives, consisting of about two thousand horse.

118 The result of the battle being as I have described, the general consequences that had been anticipated on both sides followed. The Carthaginians by this action became at once masters of almost all the rest of the coast, Tarentum immediately surrendering, while Argyrippa and some Campanian towns invited Hannibal to come to them, and the eyes of all were now turned to the Carthaginians, who had great hopes of even taking Rome itself at the first assault. The Romans on their part owing to this defeat at once abandoned all hope of retaining their supremacy in Italy, and were in the greatest fear about their own safety and that of Rome, expecting Hannibal every moment to appear. It seemed indeed as if Fortune were taking part against them in their struggle with adversity and meant to fill the cup to overflowing; for but a few days afterwards, while the city was yet panic-stricken, the commander they had sent to Cisalpine Gaul was surprised by the Celts in an ambush and he and his force utterly destroyed. Yet the Senate neglected no means in its power, but exhorted and encouraged the populace, strengthened the defences of the city, and deliberated on the situation with manly coolness. And subsequent events made this manifest. For though the Romans were now incontestably beaten and their military reputation shattered, yet by the peculiar virtues of their constitution and by wise counsel they not only recovered their supremacy in Italy and afterwards defeated the Carthaginians, but in a few years made themselves masters of the whole world.

I therefore end this Book at this point, having now described the events in Spain and Italy that occurred in the 140th Olympiad. When I have brought down the history of Greece in the same Olympiad to the same date, I shall pause to premise to the rest of the history a separate account of the Roman constitution; for I think that a description of it is not only germane to the whole scheme of my work, but will be of great service to students and practical statesmen for forming or reforming other constitutions.

ABOUT THE AUTHOR

Dr Hutan Ashrafian, BSc Hons, MBBS, MRCS, MBA, PhD is a scientist, surgeon, philosopher and historian.

He is currently lecturer in surgery at Imperial College London and senior surgeon registrar at Chelsea and Westminster Hospital in London. Awarded the Arris and Gale Lectureship by the Royal College of Surgeons of England and the Hunterian Prize, he leads a team focusing on the development of innovative technological, pharmaceutical and economic strategies to resolve the global healthcare burden of obesity, metabolic syndrome and cancer.

His historical and paleopathological work spans the classical era exploring preeminent leadership styles notable in Alexander the Great, Xenophon, Hannibal Barca and Julius Caesar. His investigations into ancient innovation include the earliest world literature from the Ancient Near East and the integration of science with art in the renaissance focusing on the work of Leonardo da Vinci, Raphael and Michelangelo. As an Egyptologist, he has offered the first pathological analysis of the Great Sphinx and his analysis of the death of Tutankhamun and 18th Dynasty Pharaohs received world-wide attention through documentaries on the BBC, National Geographic and the Smithsonian Channel. He is founder and executive chair of the Institute of Civilisation.